Welcome To The Banquet

Table of Contents

Welcome To The Banquet

By

Amy Cullum

Accepting one invitation can fill a hunger

inside of you that you never knew you had

© Amy Cullum

This book is dedicated to Jesus.

Thank You for chasing me all of these years

and never stopping.

Prologue

John 6:35 "Then Jesus declared, "I am the bread of life. Whoever comes to me will never go hungry, and whoever believes in me will never be thirsty."

It might be that you are a seasoned believer, having been blessed by God and His Word for decades. Welcome. Perhaps you have wondered about Jesus and what role He might play in your life, having never studied the Bible or been to church. Welcome. Maybe, just maybe, you are part of a growing number of Christians that have become disillusioned by the events of the world, the crime, the unjust rewards or punishments of others, and you need to have a fresh take on the power of God that is available to us each day. Welcome.

The banquet table of the Lord is rich in its splendor. There is a seat at the table of this feast for each of us. It is for each to know the ability that God has to provide for every need you have in your life no matter the event. There is constant help available. The way that the Lord sets before us a bountiful feast needs to be unlocked. What happened to the times as in Nehemiah when the Word of God would be read for hours on end? And the prayers of the people would be uttered for the same amount of time? It is not that we need God less. It is that we have not seen His power in giving Him our all, first. In the pages that follow, you will see life unfold. You will see headaches and hallelujahs all in the same text. And I will allow you to see that He is a Master at every detail, even if we choose not to elevate Him to this in our lives. Nothing is overlooked. Through sin, deepest regret, joy, humor, and honesty, may you turn page by page and see that God is for us. That God wants His promises to be new each day, even for old believers.

You need not split a meal or split the bill at this banquet. Full enjoyment is yours for the taking. Hunger, except for Christ, will dissolve. Complete satisfaction is available and ready for you in devouring the concept of what it means to fully commit to dining with the King. It is an exciting adventure for sure. He guides, and He provides. Pull up a chair. Welcome to the banquet.

INTRODUCTION

Isaiah 25:6 "On this mountain, the Lord Almighty will prepare a feast of rich food for all peoples, a banquet of aged wine, the best of meats, and the finest of wines.

Sometimes, I get so anxious that the keys won't fly fast enough when I write. I visualize each of you reading and want to see a few things happen. I want to see your eyebrows go together and think about the issue that I have raised. I want to see your mouth smile, and I want to see you clench your fist and, with a triumphant shout, say," Yes! I can make it through these trials in my life and have a great day because of Jesus and his promises!"

No one loves a smile, a hug, or a party more than I do. I find so much joy in giving parties, hugs, and smiles and receiving an invitation or hug. Smiles and hugs are contagious. But there are times when others just do not have that joy to share. The table before them is bare and stark because of circumstances and leftover crumbs from dishes that were supposed to be filling. Only God's banquet table can completely satisfy. He is the only person who can constantly encourage us through His love and His Word. The banquet that is before us in the life of a believer is indeed richer and finer than anything that we could ever experience on earth. When God feeds us through His promises, we will be satisfied with the best bites. During my life as a prom sponsor, Spanish Club fiesta host, and many different events I have worked on, I have understood what it is like to put a banquet together. There are many other aspects. Coordination is needed in many stages, including the preparation and the cleanup. And always is the letdown. The event is over, and we wonder what is next? Not so with the banquet that the Lord prepares. His door is never shut, and we do not have to worry about where the next event will occur. He has that all under control. That is why Welcome to the Banquet was written because I learned that when Jesus hosts the event, there is always a well-prepared feast.

In verses 16 and 17 of 2 Thessalonians chapter two, there are the words that explain my writing: "May our Lord Jesus Christ Himself and God our Father, who loved us and by his grace gave us eternal encouragement and good hope, encourage your hearts and strengthen you in every good deed and word." I think the whole verse would be too long to use for a title for my book or my writings, so I have just shortened it to Welcome to the Banquet.

Take one more look at the words in the verse above. It brings to mind two words: eternal encouragement.

Through our Lord Jesus Christ and God our Father, we can receive the best hope each day. This hope is only for one reason: because He loves us and saved us when we did not deserve it—eternal encouragement. No matter how funny my writings may be or how many books I write, I cannot give this promise. God can. He alone is to be trusted and praised for His goodness to us. Rejoice!

I might as well face this head-on. There will be a theme of food in this book: some struggles, some answers, some revelations. But food has been a major part of my life-technically, it is for us all! It started from the beginning of my life when I had to share the food in the womb. I am an identical twin. They didn't know this until the birth of my twin, Abby. You see, my brother Greg was a ten-pounder all by himself, so when mom was pregnant with us, they didn't think a thing about how big mom became with the pregnancy. The way I heard it growing up was that the two of us were not situated side-by-side in the womb, but me, in front of Abby, so they never heard her heartbeat. That food war I won. Abby says I stole her nutrients. So began a love-hate relationship with food. This relationship with food would ebb and flow for me throughout my life. There were times when my food was my friend, and there were times when food was my arch-nemesis. Depending on the stage I was in, I would ride the wave to whatever event was next. And just like mentioned before, many times, my table came up empty of nourishment. Many of our life stages can be seen as an event, so welcome to the banquet.

(My Motivational Monday writings will be in *italicized* print. All scripture, unless noted, is from the New International Version of the Bible)

Chapter 1- Come as You Are

Luke 14:13- "But when you give a feast,

invite the poor, the crippled, the lame, the

blind,"

It is the most frequently asked question that I get from
students and adults who want to know how to make a
change in their life. They want to follow Jesus, but they feel
they have so many things that are bad there is no way that
Jesus could accept them. Nothing could be farther from the
truth. I have come fat, thin, obedient, sinful, angry, and
wrong to Jesus. I have come crying, shouting, but also
worshiping. Jesus wants us just where we are.

Take a look briefly at the calling of his disciples.
James and John were found working with their everyday

trade. Matthew as well. Go ahead and think about it. There are many who found their lives in a wreck when Jesus called them. We all are a wreck in some manner. And if you don't think you are, perhaps this is the worst of the offenses. My story of transformation under the guidance of God is simply that; transformation under the guidance of God. Little by little, bit by bit, Jesus got ahold of me. And it was not an earth-shattering event that caused this to happen. It was because of a Savior who chased me. I would go off on my own trail too often only to find out that my way failed. It may have seemed that for a while it was working, but in the end, the results were the same. My way did not last. My plan left me farther from God and the way He wanted me to live. God chased me by, first and foremost, His gentleness. The sweet sound of his non-condemning voice kept after me. It was not as if He was a cruel taskmaster; it was as if He was my best friend, simply telling me that I could do better. That I was selling myself short. He was right. I praise God that today He still does this. It is not as if because I have solved some things in my life, He now lets me go. He follows closer than ever. Such

Many times I ran away. Other times I felt, as those mentioned above, that He only wanted me if I were doing good things. Behaving. You will read that there are many times I was not. God chasing after us happens throughout our lives. We may choose to run away from Him or draw near to Him. He loves us so much that He will continue to chase us until we are caught by his love. Trail after trail, trial after trial, God continued to mold me and still does. I can finally say that I came as I was to Him, and He took it from there. Do I wish that I had come sooner? Differently? More emphatically? No. I trust Him to work just as He said He would. Giving what I needed. Loving me all the way.

[Philippians 4:19]. I like to paraphrase it simply- God's got this. And He does.

Banquet Hall

It was one summer at a Fellowship of Christian Athletes (FCA) camp, and I knew that I needed to meet one on one with the Lord. I tried and tried to find a quiet place, but students were almost everywhere. Finally, God led me to an empty banquet room. Those are the rooms like a hotel has to host a convention. I went in timidly and turned on one set of lights to find most of the tables had been turned up and broken down, and the room was pretty stark. I began to pray for guidance and for the words of my heart to be humble as I got before God.

The scripture for my study that day was Psalm 25. I have come to love this Psalm. Verse by verse began to lay out the thoughts of my heart. I am prayerful that you will know

the grace of God that extends to all of us in the scripture.

Verse 1 ... "I lift up my soul."

 I had poured it all out before the Lord.

Verse 2... "do not let my enemies triumph over me."

 Our enemies are real, but SO IS OUR GOD!

Verse 3a... "No one whose hope is in You will ever be put to

shame."

 Thank God for his cleansing blood.

Verse 4..." Show me Your ways, O Lord, teach me Your

paths."

 It's ok to come before the Lord and make a request

for knowledge.

verse 5..."Guide me in your truth, for my hope is in you. "

 Not my ability or accomplishments.

verse 8… *"Good and upright is the Lord; therefore, He instructs sinners in his ways."*

Though I am evil- He still helps! That is love!

Verse 11... *"For the sake of Your name, O Lord. "*

This renewal isn't about me. It's about God. Getting Him into the seat of honor.

verse 15…*"My eyes are ever on the Lord, for only He will release me from the snare."*

God alone changes a life.

Verse 21… *"May integrity and uprightness protect me because my hope is in You."*

Focus on Him.

Welcome to the banquet. The hall is empty, but He will set the table, decorations, music, food, and fellowship for a life that will only honor Him if we let Him in to be our coordinator. The next time you see an empty space, I hope you recall that it is ok to come bare to the Lord. We must *learn to allow Him to fill our needs. After all, He is quite the*

event planner. (03.08.10)

Much of our lives can be seen as a banquet with different courses. God only asks that we come to Him just as we are. Broken, struggling, sinful, joyful, on our best day and on our worst day.   Many days, this described me. Perhaps you see yourself as well. Come as you are to Him. Take a hold of God's promises.

I.T.Y.L

Lord, I don't have it, but ITYL. Right now, Lord, I feel overwhelmed with responsibilities, but you knew the greatness of a task before you as well- and trusted the Father for your strength, so ITYL. I know that you will carry me. I thank you for giving me the privilege of prayer and the power of the Word. Your Word promises strength and light and hope. Help me today and always cling to NOTHING other than that, your Word. Thank you, Lord, for listening. Above all, I Trust You Lord- I TRUST YOU LORD- I T Y L- to know how things will get done. Thank you for allowing your Holy Spirit as the comforter and strength that I need. Thank you for the friends that you have lovingly provided on earth to remind me of the gifts that you give every day. You always know just what I need. When I leave this as my motto, I Trust You, Lord. I have no fear. Psalm 31:14, "But I trust in You, O Lord. I say, You are my God." (03.10.08)

What room in your life right now feels empty? How have you been letting anything but Jesus fill that space? Right now as you hold this book, is the best time to invite Jesus first to your vacancy.

Chapter 2 - The Invitation

Revelation 19:9 "And the angel said to me, "Write this: Blessed are those who are invited to the marriage supper of the Lamb." And he said to me, "These are the true words of God."

When I was eleven, I found an invitation to the best party ever, the family of God. I was baptized in a pond with fish swimming around me, and though I did not have a beard like John the Baptist- [that would come later in life with age!] I felt like a New Testament character. Being in the church wasn't new. My family was raised in the church. I began singing with Abby at age 6 in front of a congregation. We were cute little twins who loved Jesus. The invitation was to follow Christ completely, but at the age of fourteen, I found myself sitting on the fence. I wanted to be in the cool crowd. I wanted to be a Christian but also considered worthy of an invitation to the popular parties. Surrounding me were many who did not live the life from Monday through Saturday that they did on Sunday morning. Crude jokes, bad language, and only speaking certain ways with certain people confused me.

It is difficult to know who you are when you are trying to be two different people. The world standards on one side and God's standards on the other. Can I drink alcohol and still be a Christian? Just what are those sexual boundaries when I am dating? Do I have to be a sullen, serious, Bible-quoting person every day and every minute? Where is the standard for relaxing those morals? I saw it in too many lives and it confused me even more. Worldliness verses holiness. That was a fight, and it still is very real to me in many ways. But the invitation to know who Christ is was personal and real. I praise Him that it still is. I began to study the Bible in high school. It did not end the struggles with life on either side of the fence, many of them were enhanced. I loved a good sermon and the insight it gave me into my life, but I also loved the parties where everyone was crazy and had no guidelines. It was as if a view to the "other side " was finally mine, and parts of it I liked. Really liked. So what side of the fence was I to land on? The call of the world can be very strong. I even remember hearing a song just a few years later from a visiting church gospel group that sang, 'get down off the fence now and prove who you say you are. Don't play the game. You just can't do it, don't play the game. He'll see right through it. So very true. I gave my life to Christ as a rededication that night and remember it as clearly as I did when I was fifteen. Even though many of my choices since then I did not put Christ first, I know I am a Child of the King.

I find the greatest gift that God has blessed me with is the gift of joy. Each day, pure joy in Him. This I have found brings more people to ask, "Why are you so happy?", It is because of His love for me. After all, joy or zeal is what I believe to be the eleventh commandment in the Bible as stated in Romans 12:11,12; 'Never be lacking in zeal, but keep your spiritual fervor serving the Lord. Be joyful in hope, patient in affliction, and faithful in prayer."

As an educator, I have had the honor and privilege of talking with many students about an initial commitment to Jesus as their personal Savior. Most of them worry about the list of the 'do's' that they have to clean up from before they can make that jump to Jesus. "But, Momma Cullum, I do this, and I do that, and I do this too," I tell them the invitation is for who you are just at that moment. It is not a plan of 'get-the-house-clean- before the guest comes to visit. It is being who you are, all of you, and taking it to Jesus. We must make sure each and every moment that we walk with the Lord that He is the one who is in charge of calling us to a commitment of change. We cannot change to be something for someone else. We should only change for Jesus. With Christ in command of this, we seldom get multiple invitations to different events. He is abounding in love for his children, and He will not allow us to get overwhelmed. This is what was happening in my life, and I believe in the lives of many believers. It is just too difficult to sort out all the invitations of a life with Christ lived in the world. Then stop sorting it out. Let Christ. By the power of the Words that He has for us, we will come to realize that the only invitation is to know Him more. Start there, and the other invitations will fall into place as He sees fit.

The fact is that the invitation to know Christ is personal. He has an individual plan for each of us. That is why He died for each of us. When we RSVP to God, there is no "do this" first list. It is "Come!" Come to the banquet that God has prepared. No dish is needed, He has supplied all the food and all the utensils too. We are fine just as we are to come to Him. He invites us every day to His banquet. How amazing is that? The Lord and King of creation personally invites us to be with Him. I can hardly wrap my mind around that fact. We can continually celebrate that invitation and honor it by daily being with Him in prayer and habit. It's when we are directed by the world side of the fence that we get into trouble.

A personal commitment to Jesus requires that you understand you are a sinner and you need Jesus to save you from an eternity in hell. (Romans 3:23- "For all have sinned and fall short of the glory of God.") It requires that you believe that He rose from the dead and lives in heaven and waits for you there. (Acts 16:31-They replied, "Believe in the Lord Jesus, and you will be saved—) And it asks only that you commit to Him personally with just who you are right now. (John 14:6- "I am the Way, the Truth, and the Life. No one comes to the Father except through me" (Jesus Christ). Believe it; they are the best three decisions you can ever make. At the moment you are reading this, that invitation is for you alone. There were no mass emails or save-the-dates sent out to hundreds to attend the banquet, just to you. You cannot attend the heavenly banquet coming in as someone's guest. You must yourself decide to jump that fence out of the world and into the arms of the One who loves you stronger and longer than anyone ever could.

Are you riding a fence between a personal commitment to Jesus or the world? Time to climb over to the Lord's side. It is the greatest invitation you will ever receive.

Chapter 3 - What to Wear

Isaiah 61:10 "I greatly delight in the Lord; my soul rejoices in my God. For He has clothed me with the garments of salvation"

During my senior year in high school, the discussion around the dinner table was, "What are you going to do today, Ding -Ding"? Ding-Ding was my dad's nickname for me. Hey, it was better than Doe-Doe- the one my twin got, so I was okay with that! I went from an Army officer to a parachute rigger, a Physical Education teacher, a police officer, and a Spanish teacher in a semester. I never quite knew where I fit in. I was comfortable camping, hiking, and being the tom-boy that I felt like I was and still do today. I was comfortable cooking a nice meal- though they weren't comfortable eating it because I couldn't boil water well. I just loved doing all sorts of things. It wasn't so much to fit into different groups; it was simply that I like many things in life. Yes, I more than once have been known as a 'jack-of- all- trades- master- of none,' and though that used to bother me, it no longer does. I have come to Jesus just fine with all the likes that He has placed in my life. Tomboy or fancy prancer.

God made me who I am- exactly like I was supposed to be. Most of the time, the struggle of this came with dating. I always felt I had to be one way or the other. Our college young adult group would go on outdoor adventures, and I would lead the way with the fun and all, but when it came to dating, I felt the guys were looking for a softer, more graceful young lady, and I was not her. Many times my feelings were crushed. Imagine my thoughts about being the 'one' for a well-established young man in my church singles group. He had it all. His own home, an established business, a megawatt smile, a love for the Lord, and ambitions for the future that I could not wait to be a part of. Tall, megawatt smile and eyes that danced when he laughed. He was the complete package for me. I just knew it. He asked to pick me up on what I thought was a date. He had a picnic planned because I could see the basket. His was a convertible, and I just knew this would be a great date. But when we arrived at the place to have the picnic, he just pulled up beside the spot and didn't park the car. I remember finding this strange. He pulled away and said, oh, I just wanted to know what you thought of the idea. I am taking _____(no name to protect the innocent) here tonight, and I wanted a woman's opinion of the setup. Wow. Talk about pain. I think that is when I became aware that I am two people in one. Taking one part and leaving another was not an option in my dating life, nor could it be that way in my relationship with God. I needed my entire being to be needed. Upfront and honest. This is how God wants us. All of us. Upfront and honest.

Here's the best thing about this. You are who you are because God made you that way. All of the little quirks and neat things about you are handcrafted by God. It isn't to say that you are never to change. We are [or should be] daily in the process of becoming more Christ-like. But be assured that you need only change to become more like our Heavenly Father. You should never change who you are intrinsically for anyone else but God. You are uniquely you. Come as you are.

Romans 13:14 specifically speaks to our wardrobe as believers. "Rather clothe yourself with the Lord Jesus Christ and do not think about how to gratify the desires of the flesh." Such a great verse to memorize and live out. Not at all easy to perform daily. How much time would we save if we did not concentrate on our 'flesh' so much? Our royal robe comes from the inside of our hearts, not what we wear.

It is as simple as this; when you see me, you will see a pair of Merrell hiking shoes on my feet. I am rarely out of them. I trust them. I hike in them, teach in them, preach in them, and am confident that my feet will stay level and dry no matter what. That's just me. But ask one of my sisters to wear them all day long for all occasions? Not a chance. Connie, my older sister, loves shoes and has some of the cutest pairs I have ever seen. She looks great in them and enjoys them. Me, not so much. It is her comfort level. Clothe yourself in Jesus Christ. He will tell you what to wear on your body as well as what to choose for the plan that day. When we wear what He tells us to, we are just fine. When others direct us, we think about being something else, and that gets us into trouble sometimes.

Are you standing in the closet every day because you think you have nothing to wear to a party? Just put on Jesus first. The only label He wants you wearing is T.H. Totally His. (Not Tommy Hilfiger!)

Chapter 4 - Place Cards

Song of Solomon 2:4 " He placed me at his banquet table for everyone to see that his banner over me declares his love. " [The Voice]

It was a puzzling time in my life. Who was I? What did I really want? Many rewards came from my hard work learning the Spanish language. This is when my major changed to become a Spanish teacher. What a reward I felt when I 'got it. Funny thinking about it now. I came home from my senior year in college and told my father two things he didn't want to hear. That was not a pleasant dinner conversation. It was four years through my college to be a Physical Education teacher having passed all of the tough courses; Anatomy, Physiology, Kinesiology, all that was left was to pass team sports and two other classes to be finished with that major. That is when the decision was made to change my major. Informing my dad at dinner that night was difficult. The middle of dinner found a performance of a well-practiced conversation. I stated, "Dad, I am changing my major to Spanish because I just love it." He said, "No, you are not," I said, "Yes, I am, and I am also going to study in Spain!" I think dinner ended early that night.

Thus began the discussion about money, timelines, and career issues. The real issue was not being a very good Spanish student in high school. Oh, I tried, but I couldn't ever grasp the grammar of the language. Spanish was my favorite class of the day, and though my parents wanted me to stop because of the C in the class, I didn't. My teacher, Ken Steeb, made learning fun, and I got by with what I did grade-wise for only one reason. I talked a lot. Some things never seem to change.

I spoke Spanish every day to my teacher and my classmates. And though I know now that was probably the roughest Spanish ever, I kept trying because Mr. Steeb said I could do it, and I was getting better. How I have come to use his philosophy in my life and that of my swim coach, Kurt Hass; Live in an Atmosphere of Greatness! I owe much of who I am as a professional and an athlete to them. They walked through a very tough place in my life with my family while I was in high school. They never stopped helping me or believing in me and telling me to believe in myself. I have often thanked them. How grateful I am that those two helped me put the pieces of my puzzle into perspective.

After the hasty ending of dinner that night, I went on to apply for the Indiana University Overseas program, and the application process was nerve-racking. I realized the plan that God had for me in my high school Spanish background because of what happened during the interview segment of the application process. There was a spoken, written, auditory, and interview that had to take place to be accepted. I did not do well on the written exam- that grammar thingy again- but when it came to the spoken part, I will not forget the words of the interviewer. "Amy, your grammar is awful. But you can speak this language!" I finally realized that grabbing every person [sometimes literally] that looked like they could speak Spanish and practicing with them had been the key to success in that area. So my place was to be Madrid, Spain.

The place that I needed to be was away—knowing and only trusting God. Abby and I had tons of fun as little girls switching classes, boyfriends, and blame because we looked so much alike. But this was my time to go. It seemed like everyone had a place but me. I was so upset about being away from my family for the first time that when I left for Spain that on my flight from Indianapolis to Chicago the stewardess thought I was going to need oxygen! I only knew one thing for sure. God would be there too. Because of the commitment that I had made to Him some ten years before, He was with me. I clung tightly to the verse in Matthew 19:29. "And everyone who has left houses or brothers or sisters or father or mother or children or fields for my sake will receive a hundred times as much and will inherit eternal life."

When I stepped off of the plane in Madrid, it was the scariest point of my life. I looked at the signs around me, and though I had nine years of studying the language, I felt as if I had landed in Greece. I could not understand anything. I was scared. I knew that there wasn't a friend to drive me home or a bus that would get me back to my comfort zone. In fact, while I was writing in my journal that very first night in Madrid, there was a bug crawling across the floor. I smashed it and wrote, 'just like this bug's life has ended, so has mine!'

Each time I would get a letter, I would cry and cry. But I knew that I was where God wanted me and I trusted Him. That's what it is all about. Trust.

Many wonderful things happened in Spain. But the thing that was the most wonderful was that for the first time in a long time, I met my Maker. I know that usually cues the death music, but it was the opposite. I could probably take you to the very balcony where it happened. I surrendered. I told God through my fear, anger, tears, and loss of what I used to know as my comfort that even if He didn't give me a husband, and I was 'doomed' to be a nun in a faraway convent, as long as I was His completely, I would be ok.

Due to a series of events that only God could have aligned, I had to come home and forgo the whole year in Madrid. I can tell you, I left crying from Madrid to come home as hard as I had cried on the way there. Many times when I have taught about Spain, I get so passionate that I want to burst. It's not because of the wonderful friends I made, or the things I saw, or the language I embraced, though all of those are true, it was because I knew that I stood with God and me alone. And that was finally enough.

It was not until years later, after I had finished my degree and had children, that I learned to listen to God. I began to choose a 'word of the year.' Grace became a word for me to hang onto. It came to mean r-right a- against-c- Christ. G- grateful and E-expectant. You must have the middle part- r.a.c -before the other two come naturally to you. It also means that in all things we can be grateful no matter how scary or difficult. Because of His love for us and His promises, we can always be expectant of His best for us. My place card was just that, right against Christ. Exactly where I should be at the banquet.

Are you wondering what you should be doing or where you should be going? Time to switch seats at the banquet table. Give God the seat at the head of the table- after all, it's not called Papa's chair for no reason!

Chapter 5 - The Appetizer

Psalm 107:9 "For He satisfies the longing soul, and the hungry soul He fills with good things."

Having been seated at the table, many are so anxious to get started eating that we order appetizers. I now realize that the things God had taken me through in my life were just appetizers. There have been, and I am sure will be, some brutal, nasty little dishes to get through. Speaking of which, I remember one appetizer I was to try in Spain, Morcilla. Blood Sausage. I wanted to try it so that I would know about the culture. Mistake. I should have known by its appearance on the plate, [can you say dog poop?] that I was in danger. I tried it, and the texture and taste to this day can make me gag just remembering it.

Many events that happened in my life were just appetizers. As a seventh-grader, our home burned down. As a junior in high school, my parents divorced. Little did I know that these lessons would benefit me as an educator. It doesn't take much for me to understand what my students are going through should these situations arise in their lives. Appetizers. Things that prepare you for the 'real meal.' In my youth, that is what many of the things that I experienced did. I can understand the comparison of a sibling because I was a twin. I can understand not having a boyfriend because, more often than not, I didn't. I didn't understand why Abby got nominated for homecoming queen, and I didn't. HELLO!? Aren't we twins? I am still working through that one.

Piranhas on School

It was my seventh-grade year in school. Abby and I begged mom to let us wear pantyhose for the first time on picture day. She agreed. Reluctantly, but agreed. You see, the 'older girls' looked so grown up in the pantyhose, and it made them seem so much more attractive. More attractive than we were with the bobby socks rolled down!

As the day progressed, Abby and I looked as if Piranhas had attacked us. There were so many holes in our hose by the time we got home; it was unbelievable. It certainly did NOT fit the attractive look that we were going for. Ah, the memories... no wonder I rarely wear them to this day!

Here is why attractiveness is on my mind this week. I happened upon Titus chapter two, verse ten, and it spoke to me. It challenged me to look at my attractiveness in God's eyes.

Titus 2:10 b. So that in every way, they will make the teaching about God our Savior attractive.

The verses surrounding this speak about following the directions of the Master and obeying those in authority. First of all, we as Christians are to obey God and be attractive to Him so that others see the gospel as attractive through us.

There is no more extraordinary beauty than living a life that is rooted in the Word of God and firmly planted in a relationship with the King of kings. If there are areas that you are not living this attractive lifestyle, be motivated in this: no matter how many times we have to start over with the Lord, he welcomes us. It is the outstanding claim: 2 Corinthians 5:17. "If anyone is in Christ, he is a new creation; the old has gone, the new has come."

Praise the Lord for his ability to accept us where we are and love us to where we should be. I have seen Jesus many times in my family and friends. Thanks for being attractive. To those of you who can wear pantyhose successfully, kudos. I don't know how you do it. It seems like every time I

do try that, I am still swimming with the piranhas. [11.05.07]

    The best part about sampling the appetizers in a life

with Christ is that nothing- and I mean nothing- is a

throwaway with God. He can use everything in our lives to

His glory if we just let Him. Why else would Romans 8:28 be

in the Bible? "And we know that all things work together, for

good, for those who love the Lord and have been called

according to his purpose." I loved the Lord and was called-

albeit to many different things- but I knew that all was in

God's plan.

    Perhaps it wouldn't be until years later I would realize

why I did such-and-such or experienced heartache and pain

beyond belief. But God knew that what I was sampling in my

youth would serve me well into my adulthood and teaching

career. He always gives us the choicest morsel. Except for Morcilla.

Are you sampling the appetizers of the world and not finding contentment? The best plate to choose from is the one labeled PC2JC. It's the best recipe ever for preceding your main course; Personal Commitment to Jesus Christ". Time to RSVP to the only invitation ever given to you that saves you for eternity and guarantees entrance to attend THE banquet - the only one that matters: Heaven's banquet.

Chapter 6 - Musical Entertainment

Proverbs 22:9 "Whoever has a bountiful eye will be blessed, for he shares his bread with the poor."

It was fun to sing a duet with Abby in church. We grew up singing in choirs and in programs. Our first public debut was in a Christmas concert for a school where four of us got to take part in different solos of The Christmas Song- Chestnuts Roasting on an Open Fire. Hearing the song today still makes me feel the twinge of excitement in my first 'real' spotlight. The importance of performing began to change around my freshman year. Athletic competitions and working outranked musical performances. It was easy to do both for our parents because Abby was involved in all that I was. During our freshman summer though, our parents had a talk with us. The wisdom that they shared helped me then and in the future with my own children. They encouraged us to find our own paths and talents. I chose swimming. Abby chose singing. They told us that we were just in the other activity to compete against the other twin. They were right. Our successes doubled when we stopped focusing on outdoing each other and tried to become the best that we could be as individuals.

When Abby got the lead as Maria in the Sound of Music in our high school drama production, she was amazing. There was no greater moment of excitement than to watch her on stage and live her dream. Likewise, she was there during my Sectional championship victory and cheered me on at the State meet in swimming. Pretty incredible if you ask me. Not the successes, but that it was fun to live with always having your own private cheerleader!

Our brother and sister were five and seven years older and many times could not be at our events. However, we would get sweet letters and calls of encouragement from them both. That tradition still continues today.

Making the decision to stop music lessons in fourth grade would be a choice I regret still to this day. But let's be honest, I became very weary of practicing ``The Frog Jumped Over the Pond" scales because I could not understand how that would get me to Carnegie Hall. So I quit. But music was inside of me, and I walked the trail of learning music by sitting and picking things out on the piano. Having continued learning from the Word of God, the lyrics for my music from scripture would come easily for me. The first songs were as early as 1985. Some had crude melodies played on the piano, some just words. But they were real because they talked about the path that God was leading me on in my life. Seventeen years later, they were recorded.

Performing with Abby would be postponed for twenty years as we were separated by states- she in Florida and me in Indiana. When we are together, we sing. She has one of the most angelic voices ever. Sometimes when she sings, it feels as if there are little cherubs floating around her. I am not that way. When I sing, I feel like there are little God-ninjas that are piercing people's hearts to turn their lives over to Him. Both effective, neither appearing at Carnegie. And that is just fine.

We have had some fun performing for sure. During our senior year in high school, the choir that Abby was in performed a Madrigal Dinner. They were looking for people to be court jesters, something that was right up my alley.

The only trouble was being unable to talk. Many people attended the banquet just to witness me being silent for that two-hour length of time. I wanted to learn to juggle so that I could pick up people's baked potatoes and toss them, and so I taught myself. Abby was in her ' damsel-in-distress' costume, and I was in red tights with a white smock on and my face painted. We had a blast. She sang, and I played!

There have been many funny times performing as well. The first time that our youngest son, Alex, ever saw me sing, he cried. It was at a funeral for my mother-in-law and during my singing of Amazing Grace. I decided to try and calm him down because my husband, Ed, was playing the organ for the service. Gathering him in my arms, he quieted down but then became bored. I was wearing a suit jacket that day, and he tried to see what was under my jacket. His hand roamed in and out of my collar, all the while I am singing. That was a tough one to get through. Talk about amazing grace.

In addition to comical performances were our weddings. I wanted to sing for Abby's ceremony. As a gift to the happy couple, I composed a love song, but she wanted to sing it. It was a good thing that I didn't sing for sure. I was so emotional about her getting married and 'leaving me' that I cried so hard while she sang my song that the flower petals fell off of the bouquet I was holding. Abby sang beautifully. They say what comes around goes around. And it did. During my wedding, Abby insisted on singing. She did, barely. She cried so hard that the song could hardly be understood. Abby was sorry about it, but I have learned to look at that time in a different way. She was showing her love to me as well. And you know, that was ok.

The verse for this chapter may seem odd to some, but God was generous in allowing me many ways to use my musical gifts. Wanting to share these gifts with others is what I sought to do. It is an amazing blessing to sing for wee ones to know of Christ, for joining two lives in marriage, learning languages, or the celebration send-off for a saint to their heavenly home.

Around 1986 becoming involved in the Children's ministry at church became a priority for me. I knew that to help them sing. I could not carry a piano around, so I went to the pawnshop and bought my first guitar. I began to teach myself how to play the guitar. This for sure was much to my family's dismay. It was a tedious process, but I was driven to learn. They threatened me. They said if I sang Row Row Row Your Boat one more time- which then took me 4 minutes to play due to 3 chord changes- that I was going to be banned from family gatherings. With practice comes improvement, and thus was the beginning of playing choruses for the children's church and songs I learned from my youth.

It was that August that I went to Spain and I left my guitar at home. I couldn't last long without it and bought a hand-made guitar in Madrid. I never really knew how much I loved that guitar until one of my students was using it in my classroom for a skit (with my permission), and the strap broke, and it fell to the floor. It was not the student's fault at all. But having that broken was crushing to me. Thank the Lord that God had led me to a school where one of my dear friend's husband was a master wood crafter. He was able to restore the crushed-in corner and make it play again.

While in Madrid, knowing that I wanted to sing in Spanish in my classroom, performing music in Spanish became a goal of mine. I worked hard on the lyrics and was ready to perform at a church. I was nervous but confident in the Lord and so I began. I guess I didn't know just how nervous until I took the first strum on the guitar and the guitar pic fell INTO the guitar. What to do? I did not have a spare pic- lesson learned– so I simply said "Un momento, por favor," and turned around to shake the shimmy out of my guitar until the pic fell out. Nothing, short of falling off the stage, could have been worse. It really didn't matter how I sang at that point. Wow. Nice one, Amy.

Spanish class silly songs that teach my students tough grammar lessons are among my favorites. My students know I sing professionally, and one year a student had a sit-down strike until I would sing for them. It lasted about ten minutes (her strike) until she knew I was not going to sing on command, and she returned to her seat. One time I did sing 'on command,' though, interestingly enough. I was in a nail salon- pretty uncommon for me- having been invited as a gift for being a part of a wedding party, I went with the group. One worker said, "Aren't you a little old to be a bridesmaid?" After informing her that I was the wedding singer and a very close friend of the bride, the nail tech asked me, "Do you sing well?" I said that I did. She then simply said, "Sing". Talk about a moment of truth when the entire salon gets quiet, and there you are in front of a challenge. So, with my feet bubbling in the spa, I sang out with the voice God gave me. Quickly and powerfully, the song rang out, and when I was finished, only one thing happened: The woman working on my feet stopped, looked up at me, and said, "I guess you do sing well." Interesting tryout for sure!

People have cried while I have sung, I have cried while I have sung, and people have slept during my songs too. Little kids have jumped out of their seat when I hit a high note, and all this has been a wonderful entertainment for my life banquet. Not always on key, but always from the heart.

SHOUT, SING, and SAY "SO"!

Sometimes, ok, all the time, the Word of God amazes me! I am thrilled at what the Lord reveals to me in his Word and I challenge each of you; if you are not reading the Bible, get going! God has his plan revealed for his people in those books.. yes, even Deuteronomy! Here is what happened. I love S's in my life; Spanish, Singing, Swimming, and Sweets- not necessarily an exclusive list, but you catch my drift. So, this morning in Psalm 66, there were some more S's added to the list. Shout, and Say "So"!

I was thinking about how I could remember where this special message was, and then it hit me, like Route 66- the old well-traveled road. This is how we should 'get across' our trip of life. Get ready. This is gonna be fun! Psalm 66: 1-3 "Shout with joy to God, all the earth! Sing the glory of his name; make his praise glorious! Say to God: "How awesome are your deeds!" So great is Your power that Your enemies cringe before you."

Can you see it? It's the map for our daily living in the Lord. SHOUT! SING! SAY! "SO"! Each day we are to shout and be joyful to God, sing the glory of his name, say to God how awesome He is and remember He is so great that He can conquer the enemies of our lives!

Thank you, Lord, for Your Word and the power in it. And thank you also, Lord, that even if we sing off-key or no one understands why in the midst of heartache, we praise you, You do. And accept gratefully.

So get on out there and practice those S's. Hmmm... pretty wonderful that Savior begins with the exact letter! Coincidence? I think not. [09.29.09]

God alone is the giver of my voice, and though I have been in some talent shows and sung some fun songs, my favorite singing is to and for my Father in Heaven. How I would come to realize in the future that the strongest song of my life had no music with it at all.

If you find yourself off tune and the song list or band you are listening to is spoiling your appetite, learn the songs of Jesus by reading His Word. I guarantee it is the sweetest melody you will ever hear.

Chapter 7- Main Course

Luke 14:15 "When one of those at the table with Him heard this, he said to Jesus, "Blessed is the one who will eat at the feast in the kingdom of God.

Just what is being conveyed by sharing my life? Here will be quoted my favorite Broadway character from Fiddler on the Roof. It comes from the part in the "Tradition" song where Tevye says, "How did this tradition get started? I'll tell you, I don't know". It makes me giggle every time I hear that song. Writing to encourage you on your own journey is for certain where God began to move in my heart that it was time to tell my story.

It was in 1995 at school that I decided to put up little sayings in the ladies bathroom for each week. It was known as "Crapper Art"! (Again, not a good title for a book!) The goal was simple: put up something motivating or funny to get the ladies smiling. After all, I had a captive audience in the bathroom. For two years, this went on; however, after those two years, sharing more than just one line about Jesus to more people became very important. And so it began- every Monday morning, publishing Motivational Mondays. As with many things in my life, this was inspired by a teacher. One of my Indiana University professors read to us at the beginning of each week. She read <u>Alexander and the Terrible Horrible No Good Very Bad Day</u> and the <u>Polar Express</u> and others. She made us think and smile at the same time. So in my classroom, Motivational Mondays are presented each week. I warn the students at the beginning of the year sometimes they will motivate you, sometimes they will make you cry, sometimes they will make me cry, But they are gonna happen. Now, many of them ask for them or remind me of them. It is funny how things have changed since beginning teaching. It started with Motivational Friday moments, but I quickly found that few people need motivation on a Friday. It is Monday that needs a jump start.

The main course found a nice rhythm for me. A job, a family, bills, struggles, and some aches and pains as I age gracefully. Never to grow up-, might I add- only to grow older. And hope. There are funny things as you will read as well as tragedy. Both have shaped a faith deep inside. More than an "If- I- can- make- it- through- so- can- you-" story, it is a chance for you to look at your life as a banquet before the Lord and see that each course He is setting out is specially designed for you.

Because of my career as a language teacher, Ed and I have been blessed to lead over 13 overseas trips with students. It is a humbling experience to have been to the richest hotels in Spain, the wonderful hostels of France, and the poorest of villages of Mexico. Each place as well as the halls where I teach reacts to two things; laughter and positive being. Notice it does not say positive thinking. Nor being positive. It is positive being. It would be easy for many to think the way to a good workout but never lift a weight. Unless a positive being is modeled, it does no good.

My classrooms have been in the high school I graduated from for one year- a dream job for sure, a rural school in Virginia for five years with my husband and I, one semester in the inner-city school system, and well over twenty-five years where I currently am. Nowhere was the theory of positive being proved stronger than in the inner city schools that I taught in for a semester. Due to the circumstances that many of my students lived in and came from, the positive being and laughter theory was put to the test.

The schedule was up at 4:30 a.m. to drive an hour one way, teach six classes of Spanish One with thirty-six kids in each class and be in five different buildings during the day. Then drive an hour home to stay in a one-room place while all of our things were in storage. Ed and I had just moved home from Virginia. Walking into the first classroom, I heard words I will never forget. A young man saw me coming and clapped his hands together as if he were going to devour a meal and said, "Mmmm, Fresh Meat!" Talk about a setup. I simply said in my best drill sergeant voice [which by the way, was one of my career options- see how

God brings it all home?] "I am here to stay, SIT DOWN NOW." He did. Over the course of the next six months, I learned more about students than ever. They all just want someone to care. Those students had hard lives. Some of them had no homes, let alone cared about a quiz over present tense verbs. Being consistent in my care for them was paramount. They depended on my positive being. Allowing them to know that no matter the circumstance in their life, they could overcome was a daily theme that was woven into the Spanish lessons. They saw smiles, and they saw the best teacher that worked for them. And it was work. Due to having a department chairperson that wanted me to teach in a completely different way than I was used to, it was work! Many of them became some of my favorite students. Though there is no contact with any of them, they will never know the impact they had on my teaching career. Listening more, working harder- and I am not just talking about the

three flights of stairs to climb for my sixth class of the day-
and constantly showing positive being.

The Best Half

*This past fall I was on a camp out with the Scouts. Many of
them are away from their moms for the first time- except
Alex and Andy (our oldest son), who are stuck with theirs- so
I give them hugs in the morning and evening. On this certain
campout was a young man named Bradley. He is so good at
teaching the younger scouts and helping out. He eventually
finished his Eagle Scout requirements. In trying to avoid an
'older scout/ your Spanish teacher' awkward moment, I came
at him from behind and hugged him gently, and he quickly
turned around and said words I will not soon forget. He said,
"Hey, Mrs. Cullum, wait! I missed the best half of the hug,*

being able to give it back" And then he hugged me back.

What a blessing.

I have thought so much about that moment. The neatest

thing is that even though I tried to do something nice for him,

I ended up being the one who was blessed. When you have

unforeseen people stop over or an old friend comes by from

out of town during the holidays when you are rushing

around, just remember Hebrews 13:2 "Do not forget to

entertain strangers for by doing so some people have

entertained angels without knowing it." When we open our

schedules for something unexpected, it just may be you who

are blessed. [12.01.08]

It was a trying course to devour. Devouring the fact

that I was in the class again helped, but things still did not fit.

My brief stint in the business world when we moved home

from Virginia without jobs left me shaky and dry. Math was a

disaster in the business that employed me, and I just missed

the students. My husband was at a bank- he didn't know if

he still wanted to teach. Toughest of all was that we were

living with his Grandma. It became clear quickly what my

mother-in-law said, "there is no home that is big enough for

two families." I began to pray for a way out of the situation.

Again, God provided.

At a conference, I saw a listing for a job near Muncie.

Having been granted an interview, staying over at Abby's

house and borrowing a dress from her, I interviewed the next

day. I really didn't tell anyone. The next afternoon, the

principal called me and offered me the job. I told my

husband, who knew of my unhappiness, that I loved him, but

I couldn't live this way and that I was taking the job. I believe

my words were, "I hope you'll join me." The circumstances

of teaching in a school where I feared for my life, driving an hour each way and living with Grandma was too much for me. Ed was shocked, I was scared, but I knew for the sake of our marriage, it was time for a drastic change. So change I did. Greg and Abby moved all of our things on a snowy winter December 27th day in 1995. My husband began to call around, and as God would have it, a French teaching position opened in the middle of the year at a nearby school corporation. He interviewed, got the job, and moved the next week. Two bedrooms in our own apartment with just my husband never felt so good.

Grammy,, as my husband would call her, would always have my thanks and admiration. She opened her home to us. In her own way, I knew she loved me. But when she was making me try on a girdle during the first date with Ed, I had my doubts. She called me a gypsy, too,

because I have triple-pierced ears. She called me large –
even though she was as large as I. The funniest thing she
ever did was to refer to me as 'she' even though I was sitting
right next to her! When interviewing for the job where I am
now, she asked me if they said anything about me being so
'heavy.' I'd finally had it. I looked at her and said, "No,
Grammy, do people say anything about you being so OLD?"
After all, she was 93 then. Grammy loved without hesitation
or reservation. Her love for her family and her love for the
Word of God was evident as she cooked daily for them and
found her richest banquet in the Word of God. I will never
forget seeing her feast from the Word by a small light each
morning around 5:00 am.

Though teaching is my career, I am also fond of
learning. Many of my students have taught me more about
giving and loving than I ever could teach them. There are

difficult days in the classroom, but I am blessed to be able to do what I do. On paper, there is no reason that I should be a teacher. My GPA was 2.77, and I needed a 2.75 to stay in the teacher program. My National Teachers Exam was just as close, and my Spanish Teacher's exam saw a repeat performance.

Remember back in Spain? The balcony of the pledging to God no matter what I was His? Indeed He did send me on a mission trip- though not as a nun- but to a classroom and sets of students to teach, to love, and in my own way, show Jesus day after day just by positive being. My love of teaching did not expire after my tenth, fifteenth, and twentieth years, it still hasn't, and I am so grateful.

Tough problems, Simple Solutions

It is simple, we can plan on things, hope for things, and wait for things, but if we are not in line with the Lord and what his plan is for our lives, we miss out on so much. There have been many times in my life when I wanted so badly for something to happen and tried to make it happen that I missed what was happening… that is a lot happening!

Let me explain. When I was in college, I felt as if I were the only person in my family and close circle of friends that were not married. I felt as if I had no one. There were guys in my life, but because I was so concerned as to whether or not they were the 'one', I missed out on what could have been great friendships.

It wasn't until I stopped concentrating on what I wanted and gave that totally up to the Lord- I mean totally- that I was at peace. I can remember the exact balcony in Madrid, Spain,

73

where I said to God, "Ok, if you want me to be single, I will be, and that will be fine with me. You know my heart and what I really want, but…[hmmm… does this sound familiar]…. I TRUST YOU, LORD!!"

Did prince charming fall onto the balcony at that moment and sweep me away to a Spanish Castle? No. I went through many heartaches and failed relationships after that time. But what was important was the peace that I felt from the Lord. I knew that He knew, and I was in line with His plan for my life, and that was all I needed.

I simply write this to you today because I know that many of you are going through things in your life that you don't understand at this time. It is ok to tell the Lord that you don't understand and that you hurt- he wants that from us. After all, if he didn't, why would he ask for everything? I Peter 5:7 says, "Cast all your cares upon Him-because He cares for you." He isn't picky. He wants it all.

May we all take time today to tell the Lord our thoughts and thank Him for never having to leave a voicemail message because his line is never busy. [04.07.08]

There is no other profession but parenting where you can go from a hero to a villain in five seconds. "Homework today is ___, or let's have a craft day" can make a class switch on a dime! I tell them that I have sung at a student's wedding, I have unfortunately sung at a student's funeral, I have had their brothers or sisters in class as well. But the day I have to hear one of my students say, ``You taught my grandmother", that may require a few days in Aruba to recover!

Each of you teaches every day of your life. You teach about what you will do with the main course that God has set in front of you. Will you choke on the contents of the banquet? Will you request a change of dish and complain about the meal that has been served? Or will you learn that because the hand of God prepared the main course for you, it must be right for your dietary needs at that time, and you will thank Him for His provision- no matter what. It is not like developing a taste for Morcilla over time. It is realizing that through His Word everyday, He can feed you the best morsels ever if we will simply learn to order off of His menu. Welcome to the banquet. His banquet.

Are you feasting on a main course that never satisfies? How many restaurants or chefs have you tried hoping they will satisfy what only God

can bring to you? Right now it is time to start

looking at the menu of the sixty-six books that

Christ has chosen and written for you to order

from. This main course is a buffet of wisdom

that is never-ending.

Chapter 8 - What Fork to Use?

Isaiah 25:6 "On this mountain the Lord of hosts will make for all peoples a feast of rich food, a feast of well-aged wine, of rich food full of marrow, of aged wine well refined."

So what fork to use? For fifteen plus years, I was doing all that I wanted. Being a mother to two wonderful boys, wife to a loving husband, teacher, and walking marathons and half marathons was just grand. It wasn't until after accomplishing all those dreams in each of these roles and becoming complacent that the experience of an even stronger pull of God on one side and the world on the other. It was not a journey away from what I had grown up knowing, but it still seemed like a fight to fit into a group. There was that fence again. From the outside, no one would have even considered this. Being active in church, leading a youth group, saying the right things in the right crowds was a talent for me to chameleon my way through anything, with anyone. It might be this way with you. You have to wear one hat with one group and one with another. You have this certain set of standards with one and a different one altogether with everyone else. Let's not even begin to think about the language. There can be an entirely different vocabulary used in certain circumstances. We need to be one way: His way.

It was in the quiet times that the Holy Spirit spoke the loudest. The long Bible studies, the leading of Bible studies, was worth nothing if the inside did not match the outside. And it did not. My language, my marriage, my personal life, my weight, the private life that no one but God sees, did not match what the world saw. Fight after fight with duality seemed to haunt me over and over so much that I simply could not make the jump to being totally God's throughout. It is maddening because you never really know who you are. It is difficult to trust that when you are the "real you" that someone is going to like all of you. God will. He takes us where we are and in His timing, changes us to where He wants us to be. Pretending is not what God does. He is real, and He wants His children to be the same: the good and the bad.

Fear is a huge part of being and becoming real with Christ. What if the group that I sell out to does not like me? What if I take the 'straight and narrow" and cannot cut it? Choosing the side matters, and we cannot mess it up because then the other side will not want us back. It is a mess! The only problem is that we forgot to look at God's side. He is not keeping score. He matters. There is a reason that First Corinthians 15:33 warns us, " Do not be misled: "Bad company corrupts good character." So here in the text is a choice I needed to make. Listing the sins that have been committed so that you know the depth to which I have fallen is one choice. Doing that runs a risk. Some of the sins are so devious and dark I cannot bear to write them on a page. Here, I ask myself, "How will the words I write affect my reader? Will they glorify me or God's forgiving grace? Confession by writing each sin would allow you as a reader to easily jump this section saying- "I never deal with that". Learning what was overtaking me and preventing me from totally becoming one with the Lord in the flesh and spirit needs to be faced head-on. Often after hearing of someone's grievous sins, I played the game. I lived out the lyrics of a few chapters ago. It is way too easy to tell yourself in a legalistic way, "at least I am not that bad." I might offend. But please don't stop reading. By God's leading, I have decided to treat it like this: I was unfaithful. The blanket that covers the myriad of sins in my life truly comes down to that three-word statement. I was unfaithful in the care of our children, unfaithful in the care of our marriage, unfaithful in the care of my body, and unfaithful in the witness for the Kingdom of Heaven. There. It´s out. It is written. Having agonized over it, it is no longer mine. It is for God's leading in your heart as He has in mine to process those thoughts.

No program, policy, check sheet, or chart could overcome what I knew to be true in all areas, and I do mean all areas. I was living a lie. I was lying to myself that I was not living this lie, and this is the deepest earthly hurt I have. Many saw it, some called me on it, but I chose to turn the tables verbally back to them and their lack of commitment to God. It made me feel better. Until the silence came again. The roaring whisper of "hypocrite" is another word that comes to my mind. Perhaps this is what hurts the most. I was not who I said I was. Pointing out their failures instead of looking at my own was the easy thing to do.

I am sorry. To those who may read this that were or are offended, I am sorry. To those hurt along the way, forgive me. Most of all, to the Lord, whose witness I betrayed, Lord, forgive me. I have cried and ached over what has been done in so many ways the count is too high. I have repented. Often. What a glorious Lord we have who comforts us at our weakest most vulnerable times. What a beautiful Savior that welcomes us to Him time and time again without criticism, only care. I always felt like I had to fit in a group. Doing this or that. Compromising all along the way. I realized by God's grace only one group mattered: His.

So many years. So many years of living only brief moments the way God wanted me to live. Giving in to one group or another 'fix' to maintain my public walk or private need for self-satisfaction. I weep as I write. This hurts. But it is real and raw. I can no longer be any other way. And I knew major changes would call for major changes.

It may be the reason you stop reading this book. What? She is not going to lay out what those sins were? No. I don't have to. I have done enough traveling down the roads of comparison to others, and "what you did was so much worse than I' that I will not be a part of that in your life. Face to face with Jesus is the place where the conviction happens. Through the Word of the Lord is where the refining fire of change happens. His furnace can heat up so quickly and fiercely that both heart and skin sear with charred fragments. Yet as raw as the open wound is, His soothing balm of deep love refreshes the covering of the body in all its weakness to an even brighter glow than before.

Why did this moment of change happen? What is the recipe? What do you eat to get this? That is what people want to know, right? How did you lose weight? Be it the weight of sin or pounds lost. What is the quick fix recipe, and which fork do I use to get the blessed morsels of a life changed? There is only one: complete dedication for complete transformation through Christ alone.

I can tell you the date and the circumstance, but I cannot give you the recipe. Only God can do that. He serves each of us His chosen dish individually. Blessed be the Lord that He does that! When life is given over to Him as personal Savior, He becomes just that, personal. And if you have done this, you know that He can become even more of a personal Savior than ever on a day-to-day basis. Not the initial saving grace that will allow us to have an eternity with Him, but the moment by moment saving us from the pitfalls that so easily gather us in.

Will the Wicked?

It has happened to all of us. We take our eyes off of our own set of woes and look at someone else's blessed life. They have no money problems, perfect kids, no visible signs of health problems. A boat, nice cars, and life is just grand. We know that is not the case in our own lives because the bills that greet us and the problems that face us seem, at times, to grow each day.

Is it wrong to feel this way? I don't have that answer. But the Bible speaks of this very feeling in Psalm 73:12 "That is what the wicked are like, always carefree, they increase in wealth." So where do we go when it gets like that? Again, the Bible answers our questions to life! Verses 16 and 17 of the same chapter tell us how to cope with this disease called 'otheritis' . This is what I call a Cullum-crumb. A word I made up to help drive home a point; "When I tried to understand all this, it was oppressive to me till I entered the sanctuary of God; then I understood their final destiny." Don't get me wrong. I am not hoping that all are doomed who are rich and thin! But I was challenged by the middle of the verse, 'till I entered the sanctuary of God'.

It's when our eyes are on others that we fail. But when we enter God's sanctuary and share fellowship with Him alone, we can find peace in the midst of despair. My dear friend Joetta Teague gave me a Babbie Mason CD a few years back, she thought it was just a loner, but I kept it [sorry, Joetta!], and the songs have ministered to me like none other. One of the songs I so love is Pray On. The line that always gets me is 'for when we call upon the Lord, our smallest prayer is heard. Instead of our circumstance, our eyes are on the Lord.'

This week may you only look to God in his sanctuary. You will find the most beautiful music, the most wonderful artwork, and the best carry-in supper you have ever had. Fellowship with the faithful Father. [10.19.09]

88

The fork that I was to use was one of the relinquishing of my dreams. A break was needed.

Are you using a slotted spoon to eat your soup? If so, you are missing the best part of what God would have for you. And you will never be satisfied. The word of the Lord is known as the sword of the spirit, and just like the sharp tines of a fork, He will use this to pierce your duality. He is the only One who will be the right fit for every meal and circumstance in your life. Depending on anything else will only be a momentary solution. Perhaps it's time for a new set of silverware.

Chapter 9 - Restroom Break Needed

Hebrews 4:9-11, "There remains, then, a Sabbath-rest for the people of God; of anyone who enters God's rest also rests from their works, just as God did from his. Let us, therefore, make every effort to enter that rest, so that no one will perish by following their example of disobedience."

After having finished my goal from age thirty-five to forty-five of completing five full marathons and fourteen half marathons, I wondered what was next for me as an athlete? I am so much better with a fitness goal. (Too bad I did not have the right SPIRITUAL GOALS to go with those over those years!). Someone who knew my love of Spain and walking asked if I had ever heard about the Camino go. I never had. This was in 2014 and so began my first attempt to get there. Training went on for two years, and all the stage was set on the fact that I was going to be awarded a teacher's scholarship to go. I did not get that scholarship. And I trusted Him enough to know that was ok.

One day during my quiet time, it was as if God told me, "Amy, you are using the wrong fork again! You have used the shrimp fork for the steak. It will not work. Oh, it might, but it will take you much longer. Live for Me. Not the Camino. Live for Me. Not the weight loss or miles you have done. Live for Me." My restroom break was about to happen.

Make No Mistake

This may be a tough one to read, but it is reality. The other morning

early I was on a walk, and above me a fight broke out. It was amazing to see the two storm fronts colliding. The sun was shining brightly on the right side as dawn broke for a new day, and to the left was a wicked summer storm with all of its fury. The clouds moved and twisted. The sun stayed strong, and the wind was stilled to calm the movement of the imposing clouds. The dark side soon overtook the sky, and just as I thought the rain would give way, the wind would pick up and move it back again. This visual display of the weather showed me a picture that is inside each of us. Each day, make no mistake, there is a fight for your soul, your mind, your attitude, and your spirit. There is only one way to make the wind subside. Stay close to the Father. The

*more tied down you are to His promises and love, the
stronger you can stand against the storms that will surely
come. I was amazed at the power of the forces of the
weather that I saw in the span of the hours while I was on
the trail alone. (Except the Creator was there as always!) It
was as if the Lord was again visually showing me His power
and the battle that He so wants us to train for every day.*

*His love, His wisdom and His promises are there for us in
every situation. The Word of God is seen as a weapon, an
instant picker-upper, and a fortification that no song, candy
bar, or workout can compare to. Why? Because this life is
tailor-made for you. God knows the plans He has for you
[Jer. 29:11] and when we draw close to the Father, we are
strong against the storm front. This is a choice every day
that we make. Romans 8:5 states it best. "Those who live
according to the sinful nature have their minds set on what*

that nature desires, but those who live in accordance with the spirit have their minds set on what the Spirit desires"
Eventually, the clouds did burst open, and at times the lightning and the rain were so scary and heavy I could not see the trail in front of me. I prayed. I know people were praying for me, and I held fast to his promises. I would like to tell you it had a happy ending, that I kept walking and the sun came out again, and there was a rainbow. None of this is true. Just as the battle in our daily life rears its ugly head again, the storms rained on me harder, and with more intensity the longer I walked. I was drenched. My body, that is. But I praise the Lord for the object lesson of the battle. There's a reason the old hymn states, "Draw me nearer, nearer blessed Lord." Because that is where we are safe.
[06.21.10]

Since 1988 we have called our home 'Cullumwood.'

Ed has a "Great Hall" which is really just the living room decorated like a castle. The Small Hall of mine is decorated like a varsity locker room. It was in this small hall that God did a great movement in my life. Indeed God was able to get the paperwork done to change me forever through the pages of His book. On January 10, 2015, on my knees in the small hall, I told God that no matter what, I would be a pilgrim for His Camino in my life. And even if I never get to Spain to walk the Camino, I would be His and that would be enough. Recognize this speech from a few chapters ago? Yes, Spain. Yes, set apart. And again grateful to be called by God. He will call you too if you listen diligently enough. He speaks to you and tells us what fork to use: His. I decided to completely take hold of and begin to sink my teeth into the Word of God as never before. Indeed it was a complete dedication for a complete transformation. The paperwork that needs to be completed for each of us is to be completed through the Word of God. It is the richest of feasts! The journey began with Him through Romans 1:1 "Paul, a servant of Christ Jesus, called to be an apostle and set apart for the gospel of God." There Is a practical way of making the gospel very personal. Put your name in the verse. It is a personal call by God to be separated unto Him. God then showed me another verse, Proverbs 84:5 "Blessed is the man whose strength is in You, Whose heart is set on the pilgrimage." [NKJV] It too went on a paper. I did not get to go on the Camino that next year. Though it was disappointing, I was on His Camino and that is all that mattered.

How precious these verses would become in starting a new journey in a different direction. The direction of being set apart cleanly for the first time in my life. Not sinless, for sure, but cleanly and honestly. Freedom was finally mine in Christ. A prisoner no longer but a pilgrim, which is what one is called who walks the Camino in Spain.

Ballerina Dreams

It was a relationship like many older brothers have with a younger sister; volatile. My brother Greg and I couldn't even ride in the same car to a restaurant. He really got on my nerves by picking on me. Now, don't worry, today, we are best friends, and I count his relationship as one of the most precious in my life. Especially when he drove me seven hours one way to Wisconsin and was my pit crew for my second-to-last marathon, that's love. But it was not all love. The following is one of those times.

As a young girl, I loved gymnastics and dancing. I still love to dance, but my children won't allow it in public, and well, most of my tumbling is done down the stairs when I miss the last step. I especially loved ballet. So one day, I told my brother that I wanted to be a ballerina, and he simply said, "Amy, you can't be a ballerina because they only make tu-tus, not four-fours!" Grrrrr. I tried to beat him up, but he only held my head as I swung at him.

That story hit me because of how this verse reads in Isaiah 41:10 "So do not fear for I am with you; do not be dismayed, for I am your God. I will strengthen you and help you; I will uphold you with my righteous right hand." Now, this has nothing to do with ballet, but the verbs and commands are as wonderful as Swan Lake. Do not fear, Do not be dismayed. For I am with you, For I am your God. Such promises He gives to help us along our way. That is the most beautiful do-do-for-for- I have ever seen! God is with us no matter what our dreams, hopes, fears, or scary realities are. His hand is strong enough even to hold a 'four four' ballerina, and I know he can get us through whatever struggles we have. Hold that hand this week and every day of your life. Even though our dance moves may not be graceful, that is His special move. Grace. Praise the Lord! [09.21.09]

I did not have to have a rededication to the Lord when my life changed to be His, I already was, but I did have to have a re-turning. In learning to listen to God, there became an even greater need to focus on a certain gift that I could give to God each day. November of 2015, God created through Abby and me a time period of what is called Lentmas. Lentmas is a consecration for forty days before Christmas to prepare for the coming of the Christ Child when you personally give gifts to God. It begins on the

sixteenth of November. Seeking to ready ourselves

for the gift of Jesus from God, we use those forty

days to prepare our hearts. Each day brings devotion

time from the Word. Below is one of those that

speaks to the need for the break so needed.

Rock of Restoration

Praise God that I don't have to start over again and again. I

simply turn the axle with Him more and more! Isaiah 30:15

states ``Only in returning to Me and waiting for Me will you

be saved." TLB

I felt my Lentmas journey today, and my gift to God was

re-turning to Him alone over and over for strength, love, and

grace. I praise Him that I did not turn away from this, but

only re-turned again. I turned the wheel of my heart to Him. I used to hate it when I had to start all over and refocus or restart. I no longer have to do that. I simply re-turn the dials into more of Him because I never walk away from God anymore. Thank the Lord. Re-turn? Yes. Being saved from sin and self takes turn after turn after turn- but not a return—a RE-turn. Praise God for his deliverance! [11.24.17]

If I am to be able to re-turn, I must only rely on my Rock, Jesus. So I give Him the gift of being the only thing I turn to for restoration. I do this because I know, no matter the area, he is able. Second Corinthians 13:11 reminds us, "Finally, brothers and sisters, rejoice! Strive for full restoration, encourage one another, be of one mind, live in peace. And the God of love and peace will be with you."

This was an amazing quiet time and focus with God. I am amazed at His goodness. An added blessing was giving

Connie and Abby, and me a rock to carry today. Most of all to be able to share my devotions and quiet time with them. I am so blessed that God is my Rock of restoration. That it is not about steps or organizations, it is about my relationship with Jesus and the position I choose to put that into in my life! Oh, the lessons He has taught me. Forgive me, Lord, for not allowing you in this place sooner. Thank you for being the person that is my Rock. The verse for today overflows with my jobs of encouragement, one mind, living in peace. It does take work. But the end result of peace and love from God is always worth the effort. Lord, it is so possible with you. Thank you. Again, you outgive. But please accept this rock of restoration as my gift. May you alone be in front- always. [11.25.17]

Should we ever stop seeking God? Yes and no. Yes, we are allowed to rest in Him. He provides the sweetest rest ever. But no, we are to seek Him constantly. Asking how we can serve Him and know HIm better should be the goal of every believer every day. If you are a person who notices dates, you will realize that the writings above are two years after the 'balcony' moment in Madrid. It takes a while to change for sure- especially when I keep walking my own way. But here is the real truth to the matter: we need to re-turn every single day. God, in His wisdom, tells us what we need to work on and why. I did not like what Abby said to me one time after I was beating myself up for struggling again and again with food addiction issues in my life. She simply said, "It is ok. Keep progressing. We will not be perfect till Heaven" That is an issue that needs to be addressed for sure. Sin does not go away because you accept the Savior. Satan fights harder. He makes sinning look even more enticing, But God knows this, and He is the strength that gets us through. That is going to be all we ever need.

Looking at the years in between the writings, you can tell that God has been gradually working on my heart. Allow Him to work on yours. Jesus works. It is our job to work beside Him with each task and decision. And through this process, come to know Him on an ever-deepening level. The only break you need is to cut away from the world that tries to draw us from God and listen to Him when He says it is time to take care of the business at hand-paperwork and all.

Paperwork

This past weekend I was in a Wal- Mart and needed to use the facilities. I went to the big stall because I like that – or so I thought. When I sat down and tried to do the 'paperwork' for the job, I wondered if Candid Camera was on me. Due to the Sanitary napkin dispenser, the handicapped handrails-both horizontal and vertical, and the ``Safe seat" toilet covers, I could not get to the toilet paper! In order to get it, I had to contort my body into a position that I was sure I would pull a muscle or fall off the toilet. Needless to say, it was comical.

Just for today, and it might just be habit-forming, sit in silence with the Savior. Listen to his voice. He speaks peace. Matthew 11:28 says, "Come to me, all you who are weary and burdened, and I will give you rest. The only way to rejuvenate our spirits is to come near to the Savior. Oh, sure, for a while, the shopping spree and the visiting of friends or eating will get you rejuvenated, but many times these can cause additional stress! Only in the presence of the Almighty can we find comfort. There's a reason the song says silent night, holy night.

Three words of motivation I leave with you today; God is able. This gift of His power in all situations is an untapped resource. It is my prayer for each of you yet today that you plug into the real Light of the season! [12.10.07]

Need a break? Perhaps you are never alone enough to hear the Lord speaking rest to you. Where are you trying to find 'the breaks'? When we get rest from any place other than the Savior, we suffer. For true, deep rest, be like Jesus. He often withdrew to a solitary place with his Father.

CHAPTER 10 - Waiter! Waiter!-

Luke 14:17. ESV "And at the time for the banquet he sent his servant to say to those who had been invited, 'Come, for everything is now ready."

While listening to B.J. Thomas from a classic Christian album that I downloaded with my iTunes gift card, the pain began. Not from all of the songs but specifically "What a Difference You've Made in My Life". Lines like 'What a change you have made in my heart', and 'What a change you have made in my life were difficult to hear. Pain accompanied the realization that my actions, thoughts, and attitudes had not shown that Christ has changed me at all. I overate, I cussed too much. I lied too often to save face and it just was not a pretty picture of myself at all. I cried harder than I have in a long time, asked forgiveness, and somehow through the winter wind, became warmed by the grace and mercy of the Lord. I was on the Cardinal Greenway in Muncie walking. The sun was shining, and I felt the Savior there, doing what he does best: saving.

These thoughts were overwhelming; He wants us, our brokenness, our hopes, and our dreams. He wants the good days and the bad. Is it time to change things in your life? What is not going the way it should for you in your relationship with Jesus or others? Today is the day. Meet Him; He'll be there. He is like the waiter that you need at a fine restaurant to guide you through the best selections for your perfect meal.

The Pickle Jar

It's funny what brings back a memory. I got in trouble for what I did, I'll tell you that right now. I found my dad's coin collection that he kept in a certain jar on his dresser. I was just sure that he wouldn't mind if I took all the quarters out. After all, the dimes and the nickels were plentiful, and I didn't think they would be missed. Wrong. He asked me after weeks of the coin collection getting smaller and smaller if I knew anything about it. I confessed. It was difficult, but I did. He was upset with me, and I felt even worse when I found out what the money was used for. Each day after work, he would put his spare change in the jar- I called it the pickle jar because it had one of those clasp lids on it like a canning type of container- and when it got full, he would take it to the bank and save it for our family for Christmas money to buy us gifts with. Ugh. Talk about feeling bad. I did.

As I grew older, I would pass by the pickle jar and laugh at how I thought I could fool my dad. I smiled at the memory of how I got the "I'm concerned" lecture. When my father passed away over two decades ago, it wasn't his jewelry or favorite shirt that I wanted; itwas the pickle jar. I have tears in my eyes, missing him so much, but what a lesson.

I was taught obedience, forgiveness, and love in that lesson as well as many others. How often we think that we can fool God. Too often, we try doing things that go against his will, only to fall in front of the Father and ask forgiveness. Difficult, yes, but God's love is never-ending. However, we must seek out his forgiveness and change our ways. Acts 13:38 states, "Therefore, brothers, I want you to know that through Jesus the forgiveness of sins is proclaimed to you." Forgiveness through the blood of Jesus and that alone. He welcomes us back after the fall. He doesn't like what we did to have to be picked up again, but he will always be there for us with open arms when we open our hearts to Him. [09.20.10]

If you were in a fine dining establishment and you were delivered the wrong meal, the first thing you would do is call "Waiter! Waiter!" These would be the first words of help that are summoned to make this change. God only offers the finest of His meals set before us. He offers these day after day. Even minute by minute. Not only in His comfort and care but in Word and His wisdom. They are all incomparable to anything this world offers. God is at the head of this fine banquet, our lives. When we offer the wrong meal in front of Him, we are doing a poor job of service to the Lord. Why only offer Him an hour on Sunday morning but not your Saturday night activities? Stop offering half-cooked food and old moldy bread. Exchange the plate you have been serving Him year after year with only half of your very best. And give Him your finest cuisine. It does not have to be five-star quality, but it has to be a total presentation for Him. We can hold nothing back from Jesus. As guest of honor at the banquet, He deserves this. At least this.

What you will find in your 'waitering' position is that if you give your best to the Lord first, all other venues will explode with joy and peace like never before. It is a matter of belief. In 2021 my word for the year was 'believe.' How this would be challenged! Health concerns, family trials, and friends aching seemed to surround me daily. My praying had to be enough, and I had to believe that. Around February of that new year, God put on my heart the words for the letters of believe;

Blessings

Exist

Living

In

Each

Venue

Eternal

Tired of fighting the good fight? Remember this. Believe. So exhausted you cannot see straight? Remember this. Blessings exist living in each venue eternal. Remember, you must believe that God can. Period. God can. There is a blessing to be gained from pushing through. It is the knowledge that we can do what needs to be done through the kingdom's power. Not our own. Well over halfway through that same year, this became my stronghold verse, Isaiah 7:9, TLB "You don't believe me? If you want me to protect you, you must learn to believe what I say."

We must believe that God is working present-day and present minute. Through His grace He allows us to realize the job we have as a waiter. I have never been a waitress before, but I have eaten at many restaurants. I can easily picture this role reversal as I deliver to the King the meal of His choosing. I want it right. I want it clean, well presented, and just what He ordered from me. Such a patient customer Jesus is! Dine and dash is not His style. He waits long and longingly for each of us.

Each new day is exciting. New hopes, new chances, and just knowing that each moment walking completely with the Savior is a blessing. Even if it is covered with tears due to the difficult times in our lives, let each of us put into practice the verse in First Thessalonians 5:14 "and we urge you brothers, warn those who are idle, encourage the timid, help the weak, be patient with everyone." This should be the daily goal for each of us as we 'wait' on the tables that God has placed in our banquet hall. Especially His. I thank God for his patience with me.

Apples and Oranges

It was on one of our first trips abroad with a group of people, and the choices for the day were two different itineraries. One was to board a ship and go to Tangier, Africa, for the day, and the other to go and explore the Rock of Gibraltar. Most wanted to go to Africa. So we parted ways with a meeting planned back at the hotel that night. Of course, the Africa group was excited to see snake charmers and ride

camels but likewise were the Gibraltar people to see monkeys and go to the top of the rock.

When we got back with our stories that night, the comparisons of the groups were like apples and oranges, nothing alike. In a way, I felt bad for the group that opted out of Africa. They simply came back and said, "It's a big rock." Ed and I have a photo with the rock behind us in the distance, and that is just what I thought. It is a rock.

Beautiful as it may be, or as enticing, it is still a rock. When I began to think about the real Rock- God- I began to see the same comparison in my own life. Too many times I make my rock something else besides God -how that must sadden Him. This came to mind because I was re-reading my favorite training verses from Psalm 18: 31,32 which says "For who is God besides the Lord and who is the Rock except our God? It is God who arms me with strength and makes my way perfect."

Notice, what the second part says, it is God who arms me with strength and makes my way perfect. This week I hope that all of us will put our complete faith and trust in that Rock. After all, why go to an orange tree when it is the apple that you want? God has the plan and the strength to carry it out. Continue to trust. It is a must. [02.23.09]

Trying to wait on the table of Jesus and serve the world is not at all what we are called to do as believers. Take the serving apron off of the restaurant where you have been employed and clean out the pockets of all the things you have been carrying with you to work. In fact, burn that apron.

Are you not tired of showing up at the shift, working harder than ever, and having fewer tips than the night before? Show up at God's restaurant, and you will see that even if He is the only one in the whole section where you need to serve, He is the most patient customer you will ever come into contact with. Serve Him only.

CHAPTER 11- CLEAN THE PALATE

Luke 12:37 [ESV] "Blessed are those servants whom the master finds awake when he comes. Truly, I say to you, he will dress Himself for service and have them recline at table, and he will come and serve them."

Places

Ever since I was a little girl, I have enjoyed keeping a journal. I remember reading them from when I was in grade school, and each night I would put 'I love _____, ' and fill in the boy's name from that day. It changed a lot, especially when Rodney gave me a stupid plastic ring under the swing

*set when it was supposed to be real. This was in 4th grade
and boy, did the journal get an ear full that night. It helps me
to write my thoughts down and sometimes just keep a log of
what is going on in my life. Many times I re-read the journal
and find lessons that God has taught me. I find prayers that
were answered. And sometimes, I write questions that I still
have. In time, they will be answered, and I write about that
too.*

*Some of the most special times for me to write are when I
am somewhere unique. I have been in Spain, on a beach,
on a train, or in a tent when the rain pounded the sides, and
these writings I refer to as 'place' writings. Here is a recent
entry. Another 'place' writing – on a chair overlooking Lake
Oliver in northern Indiana with a cup of coffee and Jesus.*

Words cannot describe all the thoughts I have when I am in a place such as this. I am humbled in the presence of God the Creator. I am surrounded by the God of peace and I am saddened at my sin and how my life at times does anything but mirror Christ. How can I deal with the mix of emotions? Simple. Know that God created who I am, aligned my life to be as such, and embrace Him tighter. How can this feeling be taken away from this place? How can I learn to sit at the feet of Jesus when I am rushing through each day? Simple. Seek out Him above all. Perhaps this is why "Seek ye first the kingdom of God and his righteousness and all these things will be added unto you" was ever put into the Bible. That's Proverbs 3:5 and 6. A road map for believers. It lets us know that when we put God first and place seeking Him as a priority in our lives, we will have all that we need. The map of His Word shows us where to go and what is right in His eyes. That is the key. Seek Him first. May each of you

121

find your place next to Him. [09.20.08]

Only twice in my life have I been to a place where I was given the option to clean my palate- literally. The first time was when I was a senior in high school and I asked my dad to take me to a really fancy restaurant so I could learn what utensils to use in case I ever was invited to a fancy meal. After all, cleaning my palate growing up consisted of a piece of chocolate or ice cream after a take-out pizza! I remember the fancy restaurant so well because all of the sudden, after the soup was served, here came the ice cream! I was so excited about this. Wow. Dessert in the middle of the meal. I could get used to this. It was not the sundae that I would have wanted, but I sure was not going to complain. My dad just laughed. He told me that it was necessary to cleanse my palate before the main course.

Oops. I got a little bit ahead of myself with that one. Oops. I got a little bit ahead of myself with that one.

The only other time was when my roommate and I were traveling in Spain. She had a friend who was highlighting restaurants in Barcelona, Spain. We were invited to go and dine with him for a seven-course meal with all of the trimmings. It was an amazing time for sure. I have never tasted food like that since. The best thing about these is that I did not have to pay the bill for either meal. When you dine with Jesus, there is no bill to be paid. Once you have accepted His sacrifice for your sin, the bill is marked "no charge." If sin has left a bitter taste on your palate, seek cleansing from Jesus. Bitter turns to sweet.

The Elements

Again I find myself looking out the window of the study hall room at school as I watch the snow blow across the field. It seems that February sometimes just goes on forever. How is it that we make it through the dark times? The cold blows, and the days are shorter. It's all about your outlook. This past weekend we had a break from school due to President's Day, and I felt that it was God's timing for me to get a long mileage day in for my training. I looked at the weather and saw that it was going to be 52 degrees and chose my day for Sunday after church. I saw the clouds but focused on the temperature and knew rain was predicted, but I had no idea what I was in for. Yes, it was fifty-some degrees, but with the wind at a crisp 35 miles per hour and the rain sheeting at me sideways... it literally blew me off the trail once... now THAT is a wind! [My sister, Connie, warned me of wind and rain that was sideways.. how foolish of me to think it was only in Connecticut!] I found myself quoting

124

my favorite non-religious philosopher Forrest Gump. You know the part when Lieutenant Dane is on the mast of the ship in the middle of the hurricane…"YOU CALL THAT A STORM!" I kept my eyes on the end of the 8-mile trek and by the Lord's strength, got it done.

I write today to encourage you to look at the life of Christ. What if His perspective on His calling in life were only focused on the cross and the suffering that He was to endure? Yes, He knew and often spoke of what would happen to Him at the end of his life, but that was to prepare his disciples. He spent His time pursuing the work of the Father, loving one another, being an example of the Father's love, and drawing others near to Him. What a lesson for us! Obedience to Christ does not hinge upon the weather, the circumstances, or the situation in our lives. Obedience is the only choice that we have if we are to grow in Him. Tough times? you bet! But inside each one of us lies the power of the only man to overcome death. The power of prayer, the Word, and the comfort of the Holy Spirit are there for all those who believe!

So, I say, let it snow or rain, or even be freezing. Learn to rely on James 1:2-4. "Consider it pure joy, my brothers, whenever you face trials of many kinds because you know that the testing of your faith develops perseverance. Perseverance must finish its work so that you may be mature and complete, not lacking anything." Be sure to re-read this! Notice, trials of many kinds, perseverance, and maturity- they all go hand in hand!

May you go through this week knowing that Jesus is there right where you are. He knows all that we are going through, and He is loving and teaching us each step of the way. [02.19.08]

The price for a clean palate was paid in full on Calvary.
Jesus suffered and died so that we can continually look to
Him for cleansing. The main course of Heaven is joy,
peace, and strength from the Lord. Unfortunately, we try
food, alcohol, spending, and chart keeping to find the best
way to cleanse our palates of the bad taste of sin. Our
better choice is always to ask forgiveness from the Lord.
Not sample everything worthless to make us feel better.
Only experience His constant saving grace. None
worked—none will. Only cleaning with the blood of Jesus
and the promises of His Word will allow you to become
totally clean. Deep down, clean. No-stone-unturned clean.
That is the only way.

It has taken me many years to get to this place. There

have been times of fear that when I relinquished a situation to the Lord down to the last minute before He would show me the answer to the question I had. There were two events to attend, and I did not know which one to attend so as not to offend any group of people. After parking in an empty lot, I called Conne, and she prayed for me. Within a minute of the deadline, the prayer was answered. He was always right on time. There have been times when my heart beat outside my chest when I came clean with the truth about a situation. He placed prayer partners and accountability partners like my quiet friend Joetta to walk the struggle with me. She and I started an FCA group at Wes-Dell, and I know the Lord put us together without a doubt. For twenty-some years, we led together. And we are as different as night and day. She is pepper- because of her gray hair, and I am salt because I am always adding a bit of flair. She is quiet, I am not. She is soft-spoken, I definitely am not. And she is an example of right living in front of the Lord, and I was not until I cleaned my palate. She never condemned, just quietly listened and prayed. I thank God for the many people he put on my Camino here in the United States to show me the example of God's way to live and His acceptance of me even when I could not accept myself. I did not get everything I wanted each time I chose the right thing. Like the teacher's scholarship that I just knew I was supposed to get. I trusted. And I got what God wanted for me, and that was finally perfect for me.

Sole Help

There are parts of our body that we don't think too much about until they get hurt. The foot would be one of them. For some reason this morning, my foot hurts- perhaps it was the

3-inch heeled boots I wore on the dance floor this weekend! No, all kidding aside, I don't have 3-inch heels, and I wasn't dancing this weekend. I did, however, just finish one of the most painful 'treatments' that I have ever had—a slush bucket. My wonderful coaching friend Deb Buennagel laughed as she filled the bucket with three scoops of ice and cold water about halfway up a 5-gallon bucket and told me to soak for 12 minutes. It's a good thing we have been friends for a long time, it was not fun, but I do feel better!

One of my goals this year is to complete my fourth full marathon. The verse in Joshua 1:3 has a new meaning for me. Let me explain. Moses has just passed away, and Joshua is chosen to lead the people into the promised land. The Lord speaks to Joshua and says, "I will give you every place where you set your foot, as I promised Moses." [see also Exodus 3:12]. I like the

English Standard Version that states, "Every place that the sole of your foot will tread upon I have given to you, just as I promised to Moses." Let me encourage you in this, whatever your life holds at this time, take comfort in knowing that God is already there. He is not going to let you go this alone. He is there to celebrate with you, hold you, and comfort you. What an awesome God we serve! One other thing about the sole, on one of my half marathons, my third, with my dear friend Christy McGuire- Osler we saw a shirt that a walker had made with her group of walking friends that said, SOLE SISTERS. Both of us loved it and determined that is what we are, both in miles and in the heart. I am thankful for each of you reading this, that God has placed us together to walk the road, and most importantly that He is with us. May your soul find comfort in this today, and may your soul stay out of the slush bucket and on the right path with God! [01.14.08]

Whether or not you have been to any fancy restaurants, ever cleaned your palate for real, or walked any marathons does not matter to me. Sure, those are fun activities, but the real heart of the matter is what God does to clean our palates when we turn our taste buds to Him. It is an amazing transformation for sure. Bite by bite, cleansing scoop by cleansing scoop, God will transform you by His power and in His time. The only way to completely taste and see what God has for us is to be clean in front of Him. Going His way, staying upon His Word, and trusting His timing, success is inevitable. Why? Because it is the Savior, we seek to do the cleansing. And He alone does it completely each time. Go to your place of solitude even now. The elements that you seek are right before you. Find that soul solace in the One who loves you more than you can imagine: Jesus.

What is the method you are using to clean your palate? If it is anything but Jesus and His Word, the sour taste will keep coming back because you tried everything but the right thing. You will need to be totally ready for the best dessert you have ever had at any banquet. Imagine a 'Sunday SUNDAE' Buffet in heaven? One with endless return trips! We have that right now. Keep coming back to Jesus. He will stick to you like peanut butter topping.

CHAPTER 12- HERE COMES THE DESSERT

Matthew 14:20 They all ate and were satisfied, and the disciples picked up twelve basketfuls of broken pieces that were leftover.

When we had desserts in our house growing up, we went big. Unfortunately, this led to being big when we grew up. With four kids in the house, we did not get the good sugared cereal; we got the no sugar. Once, my brother Greg was asked what he wanted for dessert. He chose a box of the 'good' cereal, which was full of sugar. When the cereal arrived from the grocery store, Greg got a hold of the cereal box, walked into the kitchen, got a mixing bowl and a gallon of milk, and proceeded to really enjoy the dessert he had chosen. The whole box in one sitting. I will not soon forget the sight! Or the anger for not getting any for myself.

Do not think that yours truly was left out of the search for the divine dessert. Over the years I became tired of sharing birthday cakes with Abby and so one year I asked to be able to see how many Reese cups I could eat in one session for my celebration. This was when the regular size was regular size. Not down to the size of a quarter where they are now! I ate fourteen of them. This was when I was around that same age. Not a worry at that age. But try that trick when you are forty, and it was as if the whole quail story from the Bible was lived out in my personal life. Reese cups in the shapes of footballs came falling from the sky in the form of an 80% off sale. How could I resist, right? My dream came true. I had the whole bag in my own room on a mini vacation. I ate. And I ate. And I got sicker and sicker. So sick, I was up all night and had to be driven home. The only thing missing was the snake on a pole, and I lived out the chapter Genesis right in the hotel room. Awful. How often have I looked for something sweeter than Christ! Here is a hint: there is nothing!

You would think a lesson would be learned about why not to overindulge or depend on food. Not so. One year in class, I talked so much about the joy and satisfaction found in Little Debbie Swiss Cake rolls that my students blessed me with 15 boxes for Christmas. Ouch. Kind of them for sure, but there needed to be a different direction for my affection. . Difficult lessons must be learned over and over and over before. Thank the Lord He is a patient teacher. Looking back over these dessert menus, I see how many times I took others down the path of overindulgence. It was not exclusively in food addiction. There were many other areas as well. Crude jokes, poor language, and actions on the edge of nasty and were all poor choices. It has taken many years to realize that what we put into my body and our mind DOES matter to the Lord. It does not matter if there is a clearance sticker on the item or not. The price paid for going against the will of God always doubles the end dues to be paid. No savings were earned at all in the end, but many lessons at the hand of a loving God.

Partners in Crime

Growing up as a twin was a lot of fun. Abby and I will celebrate our 43rd birthday very soon, and though we have not seen each other for a while, I have memories of our 'crime spree' that will last a lifetime. Let me explain. It was [is!] fun to be a twin. You always have a best friend to hang out with; you laugh at the same things and share so many of the same likes and dislikes. To this day, it astounds both her and me how similar we are. We might start using the same toothpaste or deodorant or coffee creamer and not even know it. I still keep an Abby list in my files because it amazes me. Perhaps the funniest 'twin crime' that we would pull is switching boyfriends on the phone. Someone would call for her. I would answer the phone and pretend to be her. We would talk awhile, say the sweet stuff, and then ask, "Do you really know who you are talking to?" We would laugh; they would not. That is just one of many. What I love about having a twin is the feeling of the closest partner that you can get in life. It has been my privilege to share the title of twin with Abby.

I bring up the partner issue because of something I came across in the Word this weekend. The book of Philippians, it speaks many times about the partnership we share in Christ. Philippians 1:3-5 states, "I thank my God every time I remember you. In all my prayers for all of you, I always pray with joy because of your partnership in the gospel from the first day until now," What a blessing! When we believe in the Lord, we join a host of other partners who also believe. There are so many times that I have depended on those partners to set me straight, hug me, pray with me, cry with me and encourage me in the Lord. On the other hand, I have been blessed to be able to share some very tough moments in their lives as well. I can only hope that I was as steadfast in the Lord as they were for me.

Here is what motivates me today, and I hope it reaches out to you; our ultimate partnership should be with God first—constantly seeking his wisdom and guidance. But our best earthly blessing is having the partnership of a believer that we can depend on.

May you take time to search your heart to see how you can be a better partner in the Lord to someone, and may you reflect and give thanks for those who have been in your life- again, pray with joy! [05.12.08]

It may take years to find out that pecan pie is not the best partner to have as a confidant and comfort. This lesson is still being learned in my life. Every time I give God the delectable morsel I seek, including walking the Camino de Santiago in Spain, I find He has an even more of a delicacy waiting for me. We do not give to God to get something in return. But God, in His grace and mercy, will bless us when we position Him before a box of cereal or Little Debbie Swiss Cakes. It causes me to shake my head in disbelief. Does

140

God verse Ho-Ho's? Amy, for shame. But it is real. And it is raw. And finally, faithful to Him.

One Letter Slip

I remember when I was growing up that brother, Greg, had a sense of humor that sometimes my parents did not quite appreciate. Many times that is how he would break the ice or help in a tense situation. I do the same thing. One time, I remember this happened when he said a prayer. Greg said, "Thank you, Lord, for the hands that repaired this meal." We laughed; our father did not.

Just yesterday, it seemed as though tradition would continue. We were visiting Greg and his family, and he stated that he was excited to give the communion medication in his new church. This time, I don't think it was on purpose! We both laughed, and I said, "Are you sure you didn't mean meditation?"

Having thought about these words, however, over the past twenty-four hours, I have come to realize that spending time with the Lord- in true communion or participating in communion is medication. There is so much wisdom to be found in the scriptures. All sixty-six books are packed with insight and instruction. Yes, even the tough ones of the Old Testament.

It talks about the purpose of the scriptures in 2 Timothy 3:16, where it tells us that "all scripture is God-breathed and is useful for teaching, rebuking, correcting and training in righteousness." What a wonderful resource we have at our fingertips to know the Word and will of God for our lives. I challenge each of you to take time daily to get into the Word of God. If you have never had a reading plan, start in the book of John in the New Testament. It speaks of God's love for us. This will encourage you! If you need some quick thoughts about life and wisdom, try Proverbs, there are 31 chapters to get you through a month.

Yes, God's Son and his sacrifice on the cross is the biggest blessing for us as believers, but because of His unending love, He also sent the Holy Spirit and the Bible to guide us. Gifts for all to partake in without limit. Get out there and discover that in His letter to us, (the God-breathed Word- remember!?) There are no missing letters. Happy Medicating! [05.27.08]

Ineffective medicating is exactly what we do when we look for other things to take the place of where God should be in our lives. There are so many times with so many instances that I chose something over God. They can hardly be counted. But what I am going to begin to tell you as our meal comes to an inevitable close is that this is becoming less and less severe as I draw closer and closer to God. The banquet that He serves us in the blessed scripture is really unbelievable. It is as if there is a dessert morsel in every bite! Picking apart the Word of God is the only way to learn the total release of your attraction to the 'desserts' that so entice us on a daily basis.

Isaiah 12

I have been at Boy Scout camp- and recovering for the last week. There, I saw the power of the Lord in a thunderstorm, the passion of the Lord in a fire finally lit, and the majesty of the Lord in the golden sunset off of Lake Monroe. It was a dirty but wonderful week with the troop. To see the excitement of first-time campers as they learn knots and

skills is such a thrill.

I enjoy being at camp as well, because I have my quiet time

under a canopy of trees, looking out on Lake Monroe with

my feet propped up on my favorite stump. It is a blessing.

The word of God seemed to radiate through the woods and

proclaim a peace that I can only find in reading His Word

and thinking about what it means. The chapter that spoke to

me was Isaiah 12. Yep, the whole chapter. It is merely six

power-packed verses, so I ask that you read it this week.

What I would like to highlight is simply verse two; "Behold,

God is my salvation; I will trust and will not be afraid; for the

Lord God is my strength and my song, and he has become

my salvation."

Many times the Word of God can pierce us to the very core.

Sometimes with joy and sometimes with sadness, verse two

did both of those for me. I took some time and realized that there were things in my life that I made my strength and salvation besides the Lord. I am disappointed in myself. It is then that I must focus on the middle of that verse- "I will trust and will not be afraid, for the Lord God is my strength and my song." He [the Lord] will never fail to meet us where we are. I believe God is disappointed in us at times, but I also believe that He rejoices when we come to Him completely. Day by day, minute by minute, trusting the Lord. Verses 3 through 6 tell us what our focus will become after we commit to the Lord, "with joy we will draw water." (Vs. 3). I love this because though it speaks of working through something, we will find joy, and it goes on to say we will "give thanks, sing praises, shout and sing praises!" (vs. 5,6). I say Amen!

Today and this week, may we all take time to sit before the Lord and examine our priorities, our salvation, and our walk with the Lord. May we renew the areas that need help and thank the Lord for his grace. Ask the Lord to spark your desire for Him. Soon you will find a flame. Don't forget to read Isaiah 12!

[07.07.08]

Constantly looking for a bigger dessert will only give you a short sugar rush. Make the choice today to stop sampling different delights of the flesh and choose the only One who can completely satisfy the sweet craving you have, Jesus.

CHAPTER 13- Unexpected Guest

Psalm 23:5 -You prepare a table before me in the presence of my enemies

Things Change

Rocks. Big garden rocks. I have moved them five times. Last Tuesday I moved them again. It was harder this time because Alex was throwing them at me when I was trying to carry them to yet again a place they had been.

I complained. He listened. He said, "things change". Then he looked at me and said- that would be a good title for a Motivational Monday. And so it is. Things change. Jobs rotate, habits ebb and flow, and for sure life can be unpredictable. God knows this.

This is why the Lord demands of us that we only seek Him. That we only look to Him because He is the only thing that does not change. I praise Him for this quality that is shared by none other. Trustworthy. Faithful. Changeless. This is who He is. Maybe it's time for a change in your life to make this steadfast, unchanging God your foundation. Psalm 55:18 states, "God, who is enthroned from of old, does not change."

Today, it's time to decide that your direction change needs the One who doesn't. Our God still reigns. (06.12.17)

Never in all my years of parenting did I imagine it happening. It's the call you never want to get. It's the shock that catapults your world for a very long time- if it ever stills. This writing of mine was posted the day after Ed and I lost our youngest son, Alex, to a car accident. I can envision the exact events. Any parent who has experienced this can.

Out of the solidification of God and Amy as one functioning unit came a guest to the banquet that would threaten to tilt my lovely setting that had been so graciously formed by God- our own banquet event- to a scene in the Poseidon adventure where the great dining hall gets turned upside down.

The same weekend of Alex's passing, we found out that our other son and his then-girlfriend (now wife) were to have their first child. These were not guests that we expected at all. Life in its rawness never is. But oh! How I could see God working in the back room of my banquet hall to prepare He and I for such a time. Many would think that if the Master of the banquet indeed is seated at the head table in the head position all would align to a happier ever after. Not so. We still live in a broken, broken world. John 16:33 plainly states it for us, "in this world, you will have trouble," just as plainly as it states the real secret to peace in the same verse; staying in Him.

So what, don't go to His banquet then? I mean, if you are going to have heartache no matter what, just go your own way, right? Quite the contrary. You learn to make more reservations than ever! Spending time with Him and committing to Him fully was the reason I made it through these events in the first place. It was the reason that I can continue day by day. Because again, it is God, and it is me, on that cliff overhang this time- not a picturesque balcony in Spain- that the reality of this relationship came into focus. When God is seated as the Head of the banquet, your view changes. And when your view changes of God in charge,

God in control, God with you exclusively (and you are completely His), the vision changes too. Let me make that shorter for you- Change the view, and the vision changes too.

I doggedly kept my eyes on what Christ was doing in these times. My vision of Him carrying me became clearer and clearer with each choice to see this. I leaned hard into his strong right arm and wept, yes, but still leaned there first.

Pain? Yes. Agonizing pain. But a power far beyond what I can imagine enabled me to help others along the grief journey. I found myself, because of Christ's strength, able to face my faults, my lies, and my past sins with the perfect love of Christ in me. Every single bite of that banquet with the unexpected death was fueled by the power of the One, who knew this type of death personally. Cruel death.

Untimely death. Painful plates full of agony were served to Jesus without merit. And He went through each one of those for you and for me.

Each of our lives holds a list of unexpected guests that will arrive at our banquet. Their coming is undeniable. Sin and pain are in the world, causing events that can be horrific in nature. But there is a Savior. He alone is able to take this guest and turn the tables on the guest itself to show that, indeed God is able. He is Sovereign. He is trustworthy.

What I would choose to feast on during this difficult time would be the foundation of my life to the point of writing this book. I would call upon the One who never let me down. I would sit beside God at the banquet table where I could feast on His Word, even if it meant throwing the guest of grief out of the seating order. And many times, I had to do just that. Sin, sorrow, and sadness will vie for first place every day that we live. We must vow that through the power of the Holy Spirit, we will let God handle this unexpected guest. At times we must physically remove the guest. Other times we simply vow by the power of the Lord that we indeed will walk the next step into the banquet hall no matter how painful. Always there is the Master, nodding His head in approval of these steps from His place as Head of the banquet.

In trying circumstances, when the unexpected guests at your banquet threaten to overtake the hall, there is only one thing to do; turn fiercely to the Master of ceremonies. He is the strongest, most faithful friend you will ever have. Finally, that friend was mine in totality. Finally, I realized what Isaiah 49:26 was really about, "then all mankind will know that I, the Lord, am your Savior, your Redeemer, the

Holy One of Jacob." Indeed, He fought many battles for me in that banquet hall. And He is still fighting for you and me today.

Has an unexpected guest arrived at your banquet? Health issues? Loss? Financial ruin? There will always be guests that are uninvited in your lives. But the Lord will defend us. Always remember that the ripples and tidal waves that Satan sends to us (or we create on our own!) will not ever overcome the words from the One who calms the seas by His very voice. Ask God to remove the unwanted guest from the banquet. It may not be physically removed, but

from the spirit, then your spirit will be safe in

your seat at His table.

Chapter 14 - The Tip

1 Thessalonians 2:13, "you accepted it not as a human word, but as it actually is, the word of God, which is indeed at work in you who believe."

Deciding to study the Word of God as a teenager was one of my best choices ever. Verse by verse, reading and writing about what God had said. I believe every word of the Word is true and God-breathed. Claiming, against great battle from others at times, that 2 Timothy 3:16, "All Scripture is God-breathed and is useful for teaching, rebuking, correcting and training in righteousness," is spot on for our banquet hall background music.

This is what has been left at the table for you. Not

only is it the salvation that comes from knowing God, One on one, but it is also the tip meal after meal to keep you seeking His menu above all else. If indeed we can claim and cling to this fact, why in the world would we not want to devour it? In the Word, there are tips that teach, rebuke, correct, and train. In the Bible, there are four tips in one! It is true that the rebuking part might not be fun, but when it is done by the Master's hand, we are given a gift. He chases us and cares enough to discipline us. How else can we know what God wants from us? We eventually have to leave the banquet hall with Him and go out into the empty halls where others gather and stay. We must get instructions from the Master Himself.

The Word of God is so powerful that just turning to the next page causes my heart to swell. It was like Christmas one year. Having gotten a suitcase for an upcoming trip, I did not even bother to look In the suitcase. There were two more presents that I almost missed because of my initial excitement! Do not overlook this fact. Do not simply look over the main course that God has to feed us with day after day because of your schedule or unenthusiastic attitude. How can you trust and hang on to the verses that brought you salvation when you gave your life to God yet not want anything else with Him now? Not interested? How about the knowledge of daily salvation? Minute-by-minute menus of how to claim your seat at the banquet of the King. That is the tip that is left to us through the Word of God. And yes, in a word God can change a day, a heart, and a life.

Take for example, a series of events that all happened one morning before 8 a.m.

Workout

With fear and trembling, I will work out not only my walking on the outside but my inside walk even more. Pressing on and taking hold! Philippians 3:14 - [NKJV] "I press toward the goal for the prize of the upward call of God in Christ Jesus- this will be lived out in my life." Along with this, Philippians 2:12 is what I claim today, "Therefore my dear friends, as you have always obeyed, continue to work out your salvation with fear and trembling.

Oh, Lord! How can I be so blessed by you day after day in my study of your Word? It is only one thing- your <u>mercy!</u> For this, I am grateful. I am moved beyond expression that my Bible reading and my devotional book coincide to exactly what this entire Lentmas journey has been about- less of me, more of You. Complete devotion to You- letting go of the 'warped and crooked generation' [Phil 2:15]- and grabbing and holding onto you alone.

Beloved Brother, (BB) hear my prayer. It is You that I want. Sold out, workout, with fear and trembling, pressing on daily- hourly- choice by choice- minute by minute to you and your will for my life. Thank You for showing me the duality in the life I live- help me to be molded like clay in my mind and life choices to you. To stand firm for sure! Oh, Lord, I will lose it all for You. Now more than ever, I see that what I thought was gained was indeed garbage. [Phil 2:8]. Forgive me for choosing trash over you. "Where your treasure is there will your heart be also" is never clearer to me than now. [Matthew 6:21] On the way to school, this hymn was the first on my playlist

Come thou fount of every blessing.

Come thou fount of every blessing, Tune my heart to sing thy grace, Streams of mercy never ceasing, Call for songs of loudest praise, Teach me some melodious sonnet, Sung by flaming tongues above, Praise the mount I'm fixed upon it,

Mount of thy redeeming love.

O to grace how great a debtor daily_I'm constrained to be!

Let thy goodness like a fetter, bind my wandering heart to

thee, Prone to wander Lord I feel it, prone to leave the God I

love, Here's my heart, O take and seal it, seal it for thy courts

above. [11.29.17]

Indeed God is so powerful that He can speak in one

word and have an amazing effect. The strength and blessing

that come from the Word of God is such a gift that you will

find yourself without enough time to be with Him. You will

want more and more. Under the tutelages of Pastor Charlie

Paxton, Petros Roukas, and Ken Taylor for many years, I

was taught to dissect and detect the message of the gospel

like never before. These men of God used their gifts to urge me to study the Word. The "intentionality" of the Word as Ken would speak of became a challenge. It was as if Ken knew of a meal that was delicious, and his tip was left on my table- eat the Word- each word of the Word. And so it began.

Listening to the Spirit and claiming even one Word from the word is the tip shared with students when they seek advice for getting through the ugly banquets where they find themselves as a guest. I tell them to cling to a word and then make it a part of your every second life. I don't mean every day. I mean every second of every day. We must have the Word of God on the tip of our tongue as if we were salivating for the best steak ever. Indeed it is the richest of bites: Psalm 119:103 puts it just so "How sweet are your words to my taste, sweeter than honey to my mouth." God aligns His Word to meet each of us in a different way using the same power of His inspired Word. This is more than your average twenty percent tip. It really is incredible.

Let's say just for a moment that I am not going to teach any different levels of Spanish in my class. No matter how long you have taken my class, we are going to learn the same thing year after year. How dreadful that would be as a student, how unfair of me as a teacher, and for sure, it would not sit right with the administration. This is really what happens when we refuse to align our day without time in the Word. As if saying, "Lord, I do not want any more from you. I am fine with the message of salvation. Thanks. That is all I need from you." And I am ok with learning 'Hola' [hello in Spanish] for the rest of my life. We walk away, not getting to know His language. Tragic.

God has so much to share with us. Do not stop

devouring the scriptures. Through the power of the Holy Spirit given through the Word of God is where life changes. Yes, indeed. The best tip of all.

What is keeping you from getting a tip on the table each day? If you were given sixty-six tickets to a free bountiful banquet, would you not rush to the hall? Of course, we would. Free entry, savory bite after bite of the richest delicacies. What is the excuse? No time? Make time. No interest? I challenge you to search. You will be given some of the best tips that you have ever encountered.

CHAPTER 15 - The Bill

Hebrews 12:3. Consider Him who endured such opposition from sinners, so that you will not grow weary and lose heart.

It is at the end of the meal, and the awkward silence of who is going to pay the bill happens. The ticket is laid on the table. Who moves first? What role do we play? Waiter? In this case, waiting to see who picks up the tab? Server?- in this case, do we serve our meal companions with the gift of paid nourishment? Or clean up crew? - where we let them pick up the bill and then clean up the non-commitment side of things and say thank you and promise to get the 'next one"?

We have a system now in our family, and it is working

well. Decide before the wait staff even comes to the table how the bill is to be paid. This procedure works, and there is no weirdness there at all.   There is another type of weirdness that may face us outside the hall where the banquet is being served. You see, all those in attendance at the banquet of the Lord at least want to know something of what is going on in the hall. Not true for the outside world. Some are downright belligerent as to how they react or put up with the sharing of the gospel. It is time to pay the bill.

We must make a decisive move to not only preach Jesus in the crowds that join us at the banquet but that we are going to first come upon an all-inclusive, life-engulfing relationship with Christ.

Not Hard to Know

When you walk down the hall in Wes-Del High School, it's not hard to tell where my room is. I have now 'gone through' three Social Studies teachers across the hall from me, and Charlie Sims sometimes doesn't even wait till the bell rings before his door is shut. I am just plain loud. I think the funniest thing that Charlie ever said was, "I close my door before Amy starts the Spanish revival over there!" Maybe it comes from being from a family of six loud people where if you wanted to be heard, you spoke up. At least one never has to wonder where I am. Just stop and listen!

Talk about a message from the Bible that is loud and clear and encourages us to be known by our faith... "I Thessalonians 1:8 The Lord's message rang out from you, not only in Macedonia and Achaia- your faith has become known everywhere, therefore, we do not need to say anything about it."

A good lesson for us. People know us by the lives that we live. Many times, mine is not a good example of Christ. And I try to work on the areas- one at a time- (I'll be busy until He comes again, by the way!)- and this verse encouraged me to really understand that we as Christians ring out among the people. We have hope in Christ, we have the promise of eternal life, and we have a God who loves us and gave His Son for us. This is a joy! Loud and Clear. Let it resound!

So this week, I want you to really pray about and work on one, just one aspect of being a better witness for the Lord. Let your faith be known to someone or in some way that it never has before. Scary? Yes, but just ask yourselves, what if the person who led me to Christ never took a chance? Chances are, you would not be reading this now! Stand firm in the Lord!

Deciding this at a younger age would have helped so much. It is a day-by-day, minute-by-minute choice to stand with the Lord. The bill can lay on the table as long as needed. The restaurant can close down around you, but each of us will eventually have to answer to the Lord. What did we do after we received the initial act of salvation? Or why did we not take ahold of His gift to begin with? Been a believer for a long time? That does not matter. We are not exempt from answering these questions when we get to heaven. We are accountable for the process and production of what we do with the banquet that has been offered to us. There are those that will want no part in the fanfare of Jesus Christ. They will creep to the edge of the banquet hall door, might even ask for a morsel or two from the table, but will walk away silently, not needing another authority in their lives. Dine and dash describe them. Sadly, the only one they robbed was themselves.

On the opposite side of the table are those who put into malpractice the idea that once committed to God is all I need. 'He has my heart, I have the rest' is a bargain I have often heard. The living goes on as though nothing has changed. Until a bill is due, and it will be due. Romans 14:12, "So then, each of us will give an account of ourselves to God."

Piece by piece is where we find peace. His peace. He will pick up the bill each and every time. After all, He paid for the banquet with His very own blood. Will He not also pay for each and every course of the banquet in our lives?

Two Word Motivation

As many of you know, I do like to do road races. I use the term 'race' loosely. I race to the finish line to make sure I

cross it, and it is ok if I am alone at that moment. It's funny

what motivates some people. One time at the Indy Mini

Marathon, a guy had a Budweiser beer can hanging from his

visor, and his shirt said, 'get me to the beer garden!' I may

have to try that with a Little Debbie Swiss Cake roll and see

if my time improves! It is amazing what two words can do to

motivate someone. My lifting partner, mileage coach, and

best friend Debbie Baldwin just has to say "Come on!" in her

certain tone, and that is all I need to hear to get me through

a set in the weight room or a marathon. When she cannot

go with me to an event, I have her voice on a recording to

remind me.

This week, I was blessed by another two-word motivation

from THE Word, the Bible. Here it is [see if you can guess

the two words!] Haggai 2:4,5 "But now be strong, O

Zerubbabel declares the LORD. Be strong, O Joshua, son of Jozadak, the high priest. Be strong, all you people of the land declares the LORD, and work. For I am with you, declares the LORD Almighty. This is what I covenanted with you when you came out of Egypt. And my Spirit remains among you. Do not fear. "

Did you get the message? Be strong. What I love about the Word is that it does not leave you guessing as to how to do that. We can be strong because of verse five, His Spirit is in us. With the power of God, nothing is impossible. Inch by inch, problems can be resolved, conflicts can be tamed, and habits can change. It's going to be a great day today! Why? Because HE is strong for us, and no matter what we face this week, He sits enthroned in the heavens but reaches down daily to help us. All we have to do is ask. My friends, Be strong in Him. [05.11.09]

God will always make sure that His Word will sustain us as we decide to follow Him completely. It is not as if Jesus only died for that one life-changing transformation for each of us, and then He exits the hall. He oversees all things in relation to the banquet that He prepares for us. He will nourish us with his faithful promises so that we can take a stand in love for those who continue to linger outside the facility of the banquet and for those who don't want to receive the invitation in any way shape or form.

Can you, this very day, say that you have done all you can to promote Jesus? Start in your own life. What actions need to be changed? What secret habits need to have the light and strength of Jesus put upon them to morph into what He

wants you to be. Does your Sunday banquet

match your Monday munching?

Chapter 16 - The Clean-Up.

I John 4:16 ESV, "So we have come to know and to believe the love that God has for us. God is love, and whoever abides in love abides in God, and God abides in him."

Many of us have hit the blahs before in life, some more frequently than others. No matter where you are now, you must understand that these times in our lives are when we really have to get all of our faith and energy together at the same time to push through the bleakness into what we know is a better outlook on life.

How do we stop moving away from the banquet that God has prepared for us? For many, schedules are the same day after day, or kids are back in the same sports rotation routine, so what now? Do we simply go through another year with the same outlook on the daily grind? What about something new? Short-time relief can be found in a product, but lasting relief comes from the promises of God. While meditating on this thought, God showed me the first step toward handling trouble. Psalm 39:7 states, "But now, Lord, what do I look for? My hope is in you." Thirteen words that bring us a promise and a challenge. The promise is in the third word, Lord. Don't forget that God is God. Read that again, don't forget that God is God. He is in charge of our lives, and His promises are good and true. The challenge is this: My hope is in You, Lord.

We must remember that when we put our hope in health, it might fail. If we put it in people, they will often fail. Jobs let us down too. But the Lord? If we have our hope in Him and our focus on knowing Him better, we will not have to look for anything in this life to fulfill us. He will.

For over twenty years, I sponsored proms at the different schools where I taught. My dear friend and colleague Tony Santino and I would plan the event. We had so much fun doing so much work with the students. We would work all semester for the big day, and when the day finally came, we spent about 6 hours decorating. The very best part of the morning of decorating for prom was when the kids that stayed the whole time to decorate got to see the whole dance hall lit up, and the lights dimmed like it was going to be that night.

One junior girl had lost her father earlier in the school year and just cried and cried about the fact that her father would not be able to see her in her prom dress. I gave her the best momma Cullum hug I could, but there were no words that could soothe her ache. It is such when we do not clean up our own hall for our Father in Heaven. We leave trash bags full of items we thought were important all around the hall. We refuse to do the tiny details of fixing our faith with Jesus in the forefront, and we think we can do it on our own. Just like I could not comfort this student on my own, so we cannot light up the hall on our down days without Jesus. For a while, something might soothe the spirit, but it will never seal the soul as Jesus can.

House Cleaning 101

When my family reads this, they will probably keep reading because they know that I do not keep a spotless house. So for me to offer a house cleaning class would be a mystery to them. I am right above the dirt danger/ fungus finder radar in my house because it is not a priority to me. We have all had our shots, so it should be okay! This past weekend, however, Ed and I were doing some cleaning with the help of the boys- you KNOW they were happy about the family activity that we had planned- and one of my jobs was to vacuum. If you have to know the whole truth and trivia about Ed and Amy, we should be a tester house for Hoover vacuums. It seems that we can go through a vacuum in six months for some reason. And we do not even have pets! Well, a few years ago, Ed decided to buy a vacuum cleaner which required payment plans. I think his thoughts were, well, I am buying a less expensive model many times, so I might as well buy a 'Mercedes Model' and try it out. So he did. I was vacuuming, and I like to play a game and see what the vacuums can actually suck up. [Perhaps this is the explanation for the death of many previous Hoovies!] There was a small piece of a cracker there, and I wanted to see if Hoovie was hungry. He was not. So, I did the logical thing and stepped on it to make it smaller, and of course, Hoovie sucked it right up.

That's when it hit me. When we try to take a look at all of the things wrong in our lives or things we want to change in our lives, all at once, the task is too great. That is not God's plan for us. Daily we should renew our faith to trust Him and His plan for even just one thing and watch Him go to work! Proverbs 8:34 states, "Blessed is the man who listens to Me, watching daily at My doors, waiting at My doorway." Don't you just love the Word of God? It's like an instruction book! We are to listen, watch and wait daily with God and for God, and we will be blessed. What other is God so great to teach us a lesson from a vacuum cleaner? Yet today, watch Him work! [05.04.09]

The clean-up committee at the banquet is really only composed of two people and a menu. God, you, and the Bible. In his promises, He encourages us to lean hard into Him, trust Him with all that we have, and see if He will not shine light as never before. My weight issues and addiction to food have been a real bug at my banquet! It was not until I read the very familiar passage of the twenty-third Psalm that I came to a different viewpoint and really began to examine the issue differently. Psalm 23:5 tells us that God prepares a table before us in the presence of our enemies. Doesn't sound like the kind of help needed, does it? So God *prepares* my table *with* my enemies? I'm out. Hold on. Look at it a little differently. He does not say that He will abandon us when we are at the table with our enemies. He has prepared it. He is with us in this! We are not left alone to deal with our enemies. We are never left alone to clean up the banquet hall of our lives. God has known what tables need to be 'bused', and He provides each cleaner and crate to do this.

A few chapters ago, in one of my past motivational Monday writings, I used Psalm 51:10. Revisit that beautiful banquet from the Lord. "Create in me a clean heart, O God, Renew a right spirit within me. " [KJV] Here is another example of how one word from the Word can change a life. 'A.' It is a singular, indefinite article. A single avenue that needs to be cleaned up and a single spirit that needs His touch. It does not say, "Ok, Lord, do that magic trick where you steal the table cloth away, and all the dishes and settings are left in the perfect place." Not at all. God creates the 'a'. He knows the struggle that is most pressing on our hearts. He comprehends the area of our life that no one else knows about. The area that is seriously holding us back from dining at a clean table. Today is the day that you let

Him lead you through the bussing process. God will teach us to rely on Him and employ His Word to do the task set before us of cleaning up our lives. With practice, we learn for life that He alone is in charge of the table with our enemies and the power to clean it up.

What are you counting on, or who are you counting on to clean your table? Ask God to help you focus today on the 'a'. He will get it done, and you will do your part through the guiding, leading, and power of the Holy Spirit promised us.

CHAPTER 17- Grab your toothpick

John 6:27 "Do not work for food that

spoils, but for food that endures to eternal life, which the Son of Man will give you."

It is an interesting question I ask my students at times, "Would you tell me if I had a piece of food in my teeth during class that was noticeable?" The answers vary for sure. Some pretend to get sick at the thought and gag. Others laugh and say nothing, then someone once let me know that they would not tell me, they would tell others so that they can all laugh at me. Nice.

I remind them that 'vengeance is mine' and that they are going to be the ones that suffer as I get next to them and that piece of chicken is flapping up and down as I speak Spanish! I will not feel a thing. The same thought pattern is explained when someone comments- and they do- about my hair. I confidently say, "If I have a bad hair day, you suffer!" Teaching has been a true joy in my life. So has learning.

Learning the important lessons of what our job is for the kingdom of Heaven is a fascinating process. Job is singular for a reason. It is only to get to know Jesus better. The reason for this is that when we do, all other areas come into play better than could ever be imagined. Never was there a truer statement. Try it for yourself. God takes care of the little details in ways that astound me time after time.

All for a Penny

The other day on a quick Meijer run for some groceries, I was blessed by a sight that took me to the simplest form of joy. A young boy was on a mechanical horse having the time of his life. His head was thrown back in elation

as he held the reins of his horse and belly-laughed as if

he were on the Montana plains roping cattle. All for a

penny.

It was then that I was struck by the thought of what we miss

as we rush through the life that God has placed in front of

us. Have you taken time to enjoy the beauty of the world

that God created? Have you felt the cold wind on your face

or listened to the leaves rustle in the trees? I encourage

you to do so. The world was created for our enjoyment,

and each day is a chance to see God's masterful

handiwork. He has completed the creation of our world,

and it is up to us to seek out the view.

In the book of Job, God speaks masterfully to Job about the

strength of his creation. It is a good reminder for each of us *that if he is in control of the wind, the waves, the trees, and desserts, he is also plenty capable of taking care of each of our needs. There are one hundred and twenty-one verses that speak of His power and authority in creation. When we are tempted to say,' Why am I in this place in my life, God? And What am I to do?`` We need to take a look at verses 1 and 2 of chapter forty for help. It says, "The Lord said to Job: Will the one who contends with the Almighty correct him? Let him who accuses God answer him!" Jobs' reply is simply," I am unworthy- how can I reply to you? I put my hand over my mouth [v.4]."*

God knows all, sees all, and if we only let Him, He will be in charge of all. Through His creation and in every aspect of your life, may you know the joy that comes from experiencing the Lord in nature and trusting Him with your life. After all, our price of joy has already been paid, not a penny, but Calvary. [01.21.08]

Go grab your toothpick and start cleaning out those leftover morsels of the empty promises that you have chewed on for so long. More money, less weight, greater fun, lesser amounts for bills. These things in life ebb and flow on a daily basis. Jesus never does. When we complete our job of simply looking to see what Christ is doing in our lives and learning to listen to Him for direction, things change. Many times for the better. In fact, over time, always for the better.

We do have a job. In his book, <u>Astonished,</u> Justin Kendrick gets to the heart of the matter of what we are left to do when we have feasted time and time again on the banquet of God's forgiveness, mercy, and life-changing ability. We are to "take an active role in sanctification. This means that we do everything in our natural abilities to fight sin and run from temptation. You are not the primary agent of your sanctification. God is. God will always supply the power you need for an act of obedience. We must re-orient ourselves to our justification, embracing the passive role of surrender and the active role of fighting sin."

Having read this wonderful book a few years ago, it was an "Ah-ha" moment for me. It took care of wondering why we look left and right to cross a street when God is in total control anyway!? It is because we have an *active role* in progressing towards what God wants us to do. Cleaning out our teeth and brushing is an important maintenance job for us on our teeth. The dentist deep cleans; we superficially clean. Both processes work together for healthy mouths. In the same manner, why do we neglect the reading of the Word and praying, thinking that all of our spiritual health will come without effort?

The Dentist

*To say that all of my dental experiences have been great
would be far from the truth. There was a dentist who put
a shot in the wrong place when I needed 6 baby teeth
pulled, - he said I couldn't cry- I said let me give you a
shot in the wrong place! And there was the dentist who
found out that if he pressed on a certain point in my
gums, I would jump a little in the chair due to the pain.
He thought it was funny and did that about 4 times. I
simply told him that if he did it again, I was going to bite
him. He did, and I did. So, we have a rocky relationship
with my dentists.*

*To continue, I have had the pleasure of having a fifth
wisdom tooth that had to be dug out as a revenge for the
shot dentist mentioned above!- and having my two front*

baby teeth being removed from the roof of my mouth
after a bike accident where my teeth met the concrete
first! Braces were fun as well, and though it may sound
like a tough road, there is one light in the stories. I call it
the gum plate. You know, the one with the pink or white
paste that takes impressions of your teeth. They put it in
a tray that is twice the size of your mouth and let it sit
there. All the while you try not to gag, and then when
they think it is set, they pull it out. And you are just
praying that your teeth remain. I actually think this is
really funny!

As I have often said before, the Bible speaks to everything,
and here is a verse that talks not about dentistry but about
how your tongue feels when going through the process
mentioned above. In Psalm 137:5,6, it states, "If I forget
you, O Jerusalem, may my right hand forget its skill, may

my tongue cling to the roof of my mouth if I do not

remember you if I do not consider Jerusalem my highest

joy."

None of us would like to go around with the gum plate in our

mouth, but that is how we suffer when we do not make

Jerusalem- Jesus- our highest joy. With God's help and the

Holy Spirit's wisdom, it is possible to make that

commitment. God alone is the one who should hold the

sovereign place of our highest joy. We often think of Him in

troubled times, but in the joy, do we give thanks to the

Lord? He should be my highest joy, my first thought, no

matter what the circumstance. May you seek that this week

and always.

Ps. A disclaimer: None of the dentists mentioned

above in the 'tough times' are in Muncie. You are

safe! [01.25.10]

Picking a part of the Word of God is our job on a daily basis. I remember when Debbie was going to have hip surgery. Right away, because of her integrity as an employee, she asked when she could work after the surgery. The doctor told her that for maximum recovery, the six weeks after her surgery, her hip *was* her job. Why do we not see what our job should be as a follower of His? Yes, the initial personal commitment to Christ is needed. But how selfish of us when we put Christ on a shelf or a certain set of shelves and declare that He will have no access to these in our lives. I laugh hysterically and tragically, convincing myself that 'He doesn't know- so it's ok". Such a fool I have been. He gave all. We must give all. But this is not like a broken toothpick that does not work anymore. The wood from this toothpick was fashioned as strong as the wood on Calvary. There is nothing that can defeat the Word of God or the strength of God in us when we set our minds to seeking the best of Christ for our lives and giving Him the best, worst, ugliest and most beautiful of our own.

2 Corinthians 10:5 recounts the place this has to happen first, "Take captive every thought and make it obedient to Christ." Our job is to take and make. His job is to see us through this process and fortify us with His ever true promises.

There are many ways to get the word of God into our hearts. One that has been so helpful is to put it in my pocket. After all, most of our clothing has pockets in it now because we simply *must* have a place for that cell phone. So why not put the very best mobile message in your other pocket- the words of the Lord? I began this practice in 2013 and have never stopped. During my quiet time, the Holy Spirit leads me to what I need to remember that day. Sometimes it is one word, sometimes many scriptures. I fold up the small sheet of paper and put it in my pocket. I read it often during the day, perhaps in the restroom, perhaps on hall duty, and often God calls that very verse to be shared with someone in need.

God has challenged me- even during toilet time- to put down the phone and pick up the pocket- paper. I have kept most of them, and I imagine a somewhat morbid but hopefully true happening in my life. When I die, I want my funeral attendees to take one of my pocket papers, not for remembrance of me, but for encouragement from the Lord. He speaks loudly through each and every morsel that is leftover from our banquet when we chew on what he has to say. So grab that toothpick and start cleaning out the corners and crevices of the stale food that you have sampled, trying to get nourishment. The real sweet treats are waiting for you to grab. Try it. Then you will see why Psalm 119:103 calls them sweeter than honey.

Mobil Miracle

Are you waiting for some extraordinary story about how God worked, and the lightning flashed and thunder crashed and the stones burned up? You won't find that in this writing. You are the mobile miracle. Do you know that each breath that you inhale and exhale is a miracle? Each thought that you process in your walk with God is a miraculous gift from the Holy Spirit? And the best mobile miracle is that no matter the bumps in the road on the earth where we are walking when we belong to Jesus, we will be transported into the heavenly realms to walk with Him in eternity. This is the mobile miracle. Celebrate that today!

There is not a situation that you will face that God is not in charge of. It is our processing of that situation that at times causes us to stumble. This past week during one of the rains we were transporting the grandkids back home after a wonderful time with them. Imagine the scene, all the paraphernalia that goes with babies and toddlers, rain, and a deadline. In we go to the car for the trip across a busy street and four stops to the driveway. I unload the kiddos and successfully hand them to mommy. As I make the way back to the van, I notice a large black square on the hood of the car. You guessed it, a cell phone. Who knows how it got there or when in the transition! The mobile miracle is that it was still there after a rainy four-mile car ride.

Our day-to-day protection and process is a mobile miracle because our God is mobile! He is everywhere, all the time. How amazing that the Lord of the Host of Heaven's Armies is traveling with us step by step and infusing us with the best roadside protection plan ever!

I'm not suggesting you try- this- at home but I do suggest you put into practice the strong reminder that you are a mobile miracle because of the God who loves you and cares for you. Hebrew 2:4 states, "God also testified to it by signs, wonders, and various miracles, and by gifts of the Holy Spirit distributed according to his will." Seek Him daily and you will be amazed at those mobile moments that happen over and over and over. [10.04.21]

Celebrate the mobile miracle today that God has allowed us to take his Word with us wherever we go. Put it in your pocket, write it on your mirror, memorize it in your mind. Mobile miracles will continue to occur.

What is causing you to not floss? Are your gums bleeding so badly when you do because of heartache that you cannot stand another thought of pain? Are you taking advantage of all the facets of strength that God has provided for you to clean out those rough places? If your toothpick keeps splintering after little use of cleaning up your life, it is time to look for a stronger piece of wood. The ones where Jesus was nailed to a cross for you are a great place to start.

CHAPTER 18 - Parting Gifts

Job 23:12, "I have not departed from the commands of his lips; I have treasured the words of his mouth more than my daily bread."

The pickle jar from my dad sits in a drawer now, the marathon medals are hidden in a container in the attic. Things once held onto as the most valuable now gather dust. We cannot let God's Word find the same fate. It was not that I never deemed the Word of God as a gift. I did. But the practice of the Word of God was more like a checklist instead of a lifeline.

The lifeline of the parting gifts when Jesus left his banquet on earth to go to prepare our heavenly banquet are what will get us through the moments when we do not know

if we'll make it through. Writings, prayers, the Bible,

solitude, the pocket papers, these are what feeds me now.

Just as the marathons and preparation for the Camino-

which is still currently going on as I write this- takes years of

practice, so does receiving the gifts of God and learning to

appreciate them.

When a relationship would go astray with a friend or a

plan did not succeed but in its place was hurt that was deep

and true. It is easy to throw this back to God with hands

raised in a "Why?" gesture. A difficult concept to understand

for old, new, and non-believers is the verse of Proverbs 16:3

"Commit your actions to the Lord, and your plans will

succeed." Why doesn't everything work out? But as the Lord

works in our hearts to turn the tide from me to He, this verse

is verified in each and every circumstance. Parting gift

number one: success is inevitable when the Lord is the focus. Failure happens, but it does not overtake. Many times, in fact, God will show that He is truly protecting us.

No matter how careful we are when walking in a neighborhood, unexpected things can happen. God's protection was sure with my grandson Emmett and me on one such walk. We were holding hands on a sidewalk in our neighborhood when Emmett, age three, and I started to cross a driveway. The driver saw neither of us as he started to back the car right out in front of us. I screamed, and the car stopped immediately. I shudder to think what would have happened if the car had not stopped. God is always protecting us.

How does it happen that He does this? It is because of His original promise made so long ago to the disciples. We are not much different from them at all. We watch Jesus in other people's lives, we see His miracles, and yet when it comes down to really putting His promises into practice, we wait for some cataclysmic event to take hold of Him. The disciples, though they fell asleep three times, were waiting to see if the whole resurrection event would even take place. They scattered. I can hear you talking, "No, Amy, I have stayed with Jesus all my life, not one stone unturned in giving Him my all ". Friend, we all struggle with something that we want to hold onto. Something in our inner core that we believe that we can solve or make right. Even if you say you do not, perhaps this is the very thing!

Parting gift number two: Jesus stays with us. Each day we must remember and recall that He is with us. God never abandons us. Ever. John 15:4 tells us, "Remain in me, and I will remain in you." This is not a discussion of losing your salvation. It is a statement that God will always be there. Author Robin Gunn quoted one of the sayings that has played over and over in my mind since I was in high school. It still affects me; 'If God seems distant, guess who moved?' So very true.

Deuteronomy 31:6 is often quoted by those wanting to help us understand that God is with us. It states, "Be strong and courageous. Do not be afraid or terrified because of them, for the Lord your God goes with you; he will never leave you nor forsake you." Situations that we have had in our lives are so horrendous and painful we might have felt that we could not be strong at all, let alone courageous. What do you do with that? It's as if you want to scream out maybe not at God- but at the heavens so He might just get the echo- "What were you thinking, God?" "How am I supposed to get through this?" "I am paralyzed with fear, frustration, and loss!" The answer is in the middle of the verse above, 'for the Lord your God goes with you. Here is the catch: are you going with Him? Ouch.

Looking back over the toughest times when nothing was going right, I was walking on my own strength. Selfitis ruled again as I tried harder to do better. It cannot be me. It cannot be you. It must be He. One God. First. Sure, you know God is up there, but too often the enemy chants and challenges our faith saying that a six-pack of alcohol is going to help you down here. Sure, you know His promises, but if I get *this* from Amazon, it will help 'down here. Oh, and let's not forget my favorite, you *know* that chocolate cake and cold milk will soothe my troubled spirit. All superficial satisfaction. I have tried every one of them and still came up empty. Until I gave Him the title: One God, First. (See Romans 5:17 KJV) Have you ever thought it interesting that only seventy chapters into the Bible- after man had made a mess of things- ok, woman too- that God finally states what needs to be done? Exodus 20:3, "You shall have no other gods before me." God will go with us, but too many times, we leave Him. Sound familiar?

Jesus tells His disciples in John 16 that unless He goes, the Comforter cannot come. Welcome to parting gift number three. The Holy Spirit is given to each and every Believer. He may be the most active part in your life of the trinity, or you may have placed Him in a closet like I did with my medals, but mark my word, the Holy Spirit is a gift you want to learn more of every day you live. In 2016 God placed upon my heart the true power of His Word in just one word. I began to pray about using a word each year and learning scripture verses, just one a month, so I could focus on that verse. Hope was my word in 2016 because I was hoping that I would get to the Camino. Wow, Amy, you have changed, huh? It's all about what you want. Tough to change fifty-one years of habit. But the learning continues with Jesus, and I am so thankful, and the next year, God placed the word Spirit on my heart.

I understand that a dove is a symbol in the scripture for the Holy Spirit- like when Jesus was baptized- (would you not have loved to see that!?)- but I have never been a dainty one to fit the characteristics of a dove. No, not that I am not lily-white- thanks to the cleaning by the blood of Jesus- I am, but a dove is just not me. A dragonfly seemed more like me. Flitting around quickly, multi-faceted, and kind of spunky! The main difference is they don't make a sound, and as you have read, I am kind of loud. Ok, really loud. There's that Spanish revival coming out again. I get so excited about things that I cannot help myself. One student got me a mug that totally described my excitement. It said, your enthusiasm is starting to scare me. I get it. I just want others to get excited about Jesus and life, and living out each moment faithful forward, and Father filtered!

God put the word Spirit on my heart, and for each letter of the word spirit, He also guided me. It now means to me; Speaks Peace Into Ready Inner Truth-seekers. I coupled these two images with the book by Billy Graham, The Holy Spirit, and a world opened up to me as never before. When we begin to study differently, we will see differently. We will process wiser than before because the Lord is leading. We will begin to pray with more direction and strength. And it is. It was all Jesus. His strength, His focus, His reward, His honor. All because we choose to work on knowing Him better. There is that tough word that folks just do not want to hear, let alone do: work. It takes work. But I have never been more successful in my plans, more productive in my time, more at peace in my heart because of this choice to get to know Jesus and his parting gifts.

I made a commitment to know verses and where they come from. My sisters Connie and Abby, and I were sharing one time about our favorite verses and one of us could not remember where they came from. "What, girl? You don't even *know* where your favorite verse is?" This became as much of a story as it was a joke and a challenge between us. We challenged each other in our study habits and memorization process. All of us have been changed for the better. The Holy Spirit will lead you. Even to study the tough books of the Bible.

And lastly, the fourth parting gift: the Word of God.

I Know

Summer. It will have to be summer before I can ever sit down and recap the events of all this spring. Good and bad. Exhilarating and heartbreaking all at once. But I know this. God lives. He reigns. And because of this, I have hope and the ability to conquer the only weapon Satan can use against me; my mind. In drawing closer to Christ, in knowing more of his Word, praying and listening, somehow the devil gets smaller or seems farther away. Notice I didn't say less powerful. Unfortunately, he becomes stronger. The pull for my life and my actions become an all-out war.

But I must quote 2 Timothy 2:12, "Yet I know whom I have believed and am persuaded that he is able to guard what I have entrusted to Him for that day."

WOW! I just read the whole verse. Above was just the 'part b'. The first part says, "That is why I am suffering as I am." Isn't the Bible a glorious gift from God? Sixty- Six books and over five thousand power-packed verses to guide, soothe, chide, and heal. It's all there. Thank you, Lord, yet again for the answers found in your Word. [04.26.10]

The gifts that are given to us by the sacrifice of Christ on the cross are ours for the taking! His presence, His Spirit, an attitude of success no matter what, and the blessed Word of God. All for you at only the cost of taking ahold of them. What parting gift are you leaving on the table as you go?

Chapter 19 - Closing the Hall

Acts 20:24 "However, I consider my life worth nothing to me; my only aim is to finish the race and complete the task the Lord Jesus has given me- the task of testifying to the good news of God's grace."

Ever have one of those moments at a restaurant where you order from your menu, and then you wonder if you ordered the right item? In writing this book, I found myself in much the same predicament. There are several books that I have been working on for many years. I did not know which one to pursue. God made this book the clear choice to me while I was in the small hall with Him one morning.

Jehovah-Nissi- the Lord, my banner- standard-bearer.

This sealed the answer to my prayer about which book to work on first. I cannot escape the title or the joy about the banquet table that God has for me. His name is a sign of hope, a place to visualize, and right now, a declaration station. From my monthly pocket paper, this was Jesus' name for today. I'm surrounded. I am surrounded by the truth of the Word, as I am faced with a teaching nightmare and a horrific schedule of things ahead of me. It is just bad. So I raise a banner as I sit at his banquet table- eating and drinking my fill of who He is and all He has for me- should I choose to partake. I can savor every morsel, or I can make each one sour in my mouth as I look to the world to fulfill and solve. It never will. Only He satisfies completely.

Just as the pages of the book come to a close and our quiet times with God come to a close, how do we *not* close our fellowship with God as we go out of the hall? As always, the instruction from the Lord is there to help. Micah 7:7 has become a stronghold for me in this quest for total consecration in front of the Lord. "But as for me, I watch in hope for the Lord, I wait for God my Savior for my God will hear me!" In this short verse, the closing of the hall instructions are given to each of us. We watch, we hope, we wait, we trust—four keys to unlock the entrance to the main hall from the banquet hall. In our spirits and hearts, we should never leave the banquet hall of the Lord, but we have to go on to our daily duties because most of us have a job to do. So we take God and his plan with us.

Psalm 69:32 NLT challenges us even further to understand that God does not let us down. That in the day-in-day-out living, God is alive and living to help us. What a reason to rejoice! "The humble will see their God at work and be glad. Let all who seek God's help be encouraged." NLT Going after God means this takes place in all that I am, and all that I do, and in every single situation I ask Him first. I fall short of this many days. But each hour, He is working on my heart to keep me seeking Him and depending on his wisdom.

I admire how God works and entwines everything that I am feeling and learning from His Word. If I know that he has prepared in advance for me, [Jeremiah 29:11] and I know that I am strengthened in his shadow [Psalm 91:4]. I must go after the places that he has for me that even though they are shadowed, and I might not understand, I am protected. Going after Jesus is hard work. There is that word again; work. We have to work to go after Jesus in all things.

John 3:30 says that "He must be greater, and I must become less." 'Go after!" is the battle cry. We must continue in our lives to let Jesus lead. We must have sole and soul dedication *to go* after Him. Not only this but we must continue to let Him shine and not ourselves. It truly is the only way that we can live happily; total obedience to the Word of God and total control by Christ—in essence, going after Him alone. That is what will benefit the most.

God gave me this one early morning with Him, and it seems to sum up the steps to success that I have to climb as I close down the small hall time with Him and exit to the 'real world.' I pray that they bless you as well:

I MUST ONLY TRUST

EACH DAY ONLY OBEY

THE HOLY SPIRIT

THE ONLY WAY

It's when I take my eyes off of Him I lose the ability to complete the tasks listed. Instead, I go after myself. More times than I can count, however, to complete failure. Sure, I think about this with my food. I understand if I will seek to please Christ on my plate and not my palate, then It will be better choices. As soon as I start going after me and not He, then it will not work out in the long run. "Seek first the kingdom of God and his righteousness" [Matthew 6:33]. That is what I want. Won't you join Him today? Nothing ever closes with Christ. He is always open to all that we are. He says welcome to the banquet. I am so thankful that I accepted His invitation. You will be also.

Thank You, Lord

Clouds of silver, line the sky

ending another summer's day.

The sunbeams over a country hill

The works of God for all displayed

Lord, thank you for the beauty of

the world that you have made,

And thank you for the life to me you gave.

I'd just like to lift my voice,

In a song of praise to you,

Thanking you for all you've brought me through.

Darkness fall as night draws near,

ending another perfect day.

Lord above who created all, in

Such a perfect way- that I'd

just like to lift my voice

In a song of praise to you,

Thanking you for all you've brought me through.

Lord, thank you for the beauty of

the world that you have made,

And thank you for the life to me you gave.

[July 1986]

Words and music by:

(Then)

Amy Anderson

Acknowledgments

I am so grateful-

- For my husband, Ed, for supporting me in my writing
- For Andy, my son, always telling me that he believes in me
- For my editors, Sonya Paul and Abby Harrough, your insight, gentle guidance, support, and encouragement have been incredible
- For my sister, Connie, my brother Greg, and my twin Abby, thank you for always teaching me by example
- For- In alphabetical order- Denise Blanton, Lori Clementi, Sue Ellen Hardley and Joetta Teague for your relentless suggestions of writing a book. Neither of you ever stopped saying, "I am waiting for that book," or "When are you going to write that book?" or "You know, you should write a book!". Thank you for your consistency- it's finally here!

To My Readers

I am overcome with emotion as I see this page being written. I am honored to have been guided by God to write for Him. It is amazing that this book actually started over eight years ago, and now it is finished. Such a journey that God gives us when we trust Him.

My hope for you is that you find the hope in this book. My prayer is that you would know God has a plan for each of your lives. The best plan that we can put into practice is to commit personally to Jesus. It might be the scariest thing you do, but it will be the most rewarding both for now and for eternity. This decision is made by admitting that you are a sinner, believing that Jesus died for your sins, and committing your heart to have a personal relationship with Jesus. First and foremost, that is my prayer for you. If that has been done in your life, I pray that you would get to know Him more and more by taking a second leap of faith - after having personally turned your life to Him- and live wholeheartedly learning, seeking, watching, and trusting the Father.

Before *Welcome to the Banquet* was even put onto page one, I prayed for my readers. As I wrote, I prayed for you, and as it is sent out and shared, I will continue to pray. If only one life is changed, that will be enough. God is always better than good, and may He alone get all the glory for this, my very first book.

Do Good Things-

Hugs in Him-
Amy C.

Printed in Great Britain
by Amazon

27350766R00126